MADISON

ENCYCLOPEDIA of PRESIDENTS

James Madison

Fourth President of the United States

By Susan Clinton

CHILDRENS PRESS ®

CHICAGO

President Madison's home at Montpelier, Virginia, as it looks today

Library of Congress Cataloging-in-Publication Data

Clinton, Susan.
  James Madison.

  (Encyclopedia of presidents)
  Includes index.
  Summary: Recounts the story of America's fourth
president, known as the Father of the Constitution,
describing his early life in Virginia and his many
years of service in public office.
  1. Madison, James, 1751-1836—Juvenile literature.
2. Presidents—United States—Biography—Juvenile
literature. 3. United States—History—1783-1815—
Juvenile literature. [1. Madison, James, 1751-1836.
2. Presidents] I. Title. II. Series.
E342.C57 1986   973.5'092'4 [B] [92]   86-13630
ISBN 0-516-01382-3

Picture Acknowledgments

The Bettmann Archive—4, 9, 21 (left), 33, 50,
53 (2 pictures), 55, 57 (top right), 61, 64, 69, 73,
78, 79, 80, 83
Historical Pictures Service—5, 11, 14, 21
(right), 23, 24, 26, 28, 29, 37, 38, 41 (left), 42,
45, 46, 49, 56, 57 (bottom), 70, 84, 88 (left)
Library of Congress—8 (right), 22, 54, 57 (left),
82
Nawrocki Stock Photo:
© William S. Nawrocki—13, 30 (3 pictures)
North Wind Picture Archives—6, 8 (left), 10,
16, 17, 18 (3 pictures), 19, 20, 62, 66, 81
H. Armstrong Roberts—12, 41 (right), 51, 58,
74 (2 pictures), 75 (2 pictures)
U.S. Bureau of Printing and Engraving—2, 8
(center), 88 (3 right pictures)

Cover design and illustration
by Steven Gaston Dobson

James Madison presents the U.S. Constitution to George Washington
in this mural in the National Archives in Washington, D.C.

Table of Contents

Chapter 1   Father of the Constitution 7
Chapter 2   The Education of a Planter's Son 15
Chapter 3   Freedom of Religion. 25
Chapter 4   Paying for the Revolution 31
Chapter 5   The Constitutional Convention 39
Chapter 6   Starting Up 47
Chapter 7   Secretary of State 59
Chapter 8   First Term 65
Chapter 9   The War of 1812 71
Chapter 10   Retirement. 85
Chronology of American History 90
Index 99

James Madison

Chapter 1

Father of the Constitution

The summer of 1787 was hot and muggy, and the first-floor room in the Philadelphia State House was even worse—full of buzzing flies and angry, arguing men. This was the room where the Declaration of Independence had been signed in 1776, creating the United States of America. Now representatives of most of the thirteen original states were meeting to face up to a terrible problem: the United States was not working. The states were too suspicious and too jealous of their own independence to work together. The central government was too weak to make them do it.

The agreement that bound the states together in the days just after the American Revolution was called the Articles of Confederation. The Articles were the source of most of the problems the young nation faced, but many people still thought that the Articles could work with a few minor adjustments.

Three men who worked to create the Constitution. Top: George Washington, who presided over the Constitutional Convention. Left: Alexander Hamilton, later Washington's secretary of the treasury. Right: Benjamin Franklin, scientist, writer, and statesman

The Philadelphia meeting was called the Constitutional Convention, and its job was to establish a new government for the United States. All summer long, as men like George Washington, Alexander Hamilton, and Benjamin Franklin struggled with that awesome task, one young delegate from Virginia never missed a session. A small, slender, shy man, he sat up front each day so that he could hear every speech. Through all the sessions, through speeches that sometimes lasted six hours or more, he took notes. He wrote down the speeches, the arguments, and the votes. Then he went back to his boardinghouse and read them over and thought them through. Each evening he wrote out arguments in favor of the ideas he agreed with and against the ideas he thought were wrong. His days were long and hard, but he didn't mind. He thought this meeting was important to America and to the world.

A session of the Constitutional Convention in Philadelphia, 1787

The young Virginian's name was James Madison, and he had come to the convention with a plan for a strong central government to rule over all the states and keep them together. It wasn't easy to get the other delegates to agree with him — it wasn't easy to get them to agree on anything at all. As the summer grew hotter and hotter, tempers flared and angry voices filled the meeting room. Some delegates became so angry they walked out for good, but most stayed until the job was done. When they finally finished the new Constitution, it followed Madison's plan. Because his ideas were so important in shaping our government, Madison is remembered as the Father of the Constitution.

George Washington's starving and poorly-clothed troops at Valley Forge were victims of the Continental Congress's money problems. One-fourth of the soldiers who started the winter of 1777-78 at Valley Forge died before spring.

Madison knew firsthand how hard it was to make thirteen states act as one country. During the Revolution, he was a member of the Second Continental Congress, a group of men chosen by the states to run the country. One of his first jobs was to write to a naval officer to tell him that Congress couldn't send bread for his sailors. Even if Congress had had any bread, there were no ships to carry it.

The Continental Congress had no money to pay soldiers or to buy food or uniforms. It could ask the states for money, but it had no way to force them to pay. And although each state was willing to help its own soldiers, none was willing to pay for a national army. Sometimes it seemed as if the states were more worried about each other than about their common enemy, the British.

Life for settlers on the frontier was worlds away from the bustling life of city dwellers.

The thirteen states simply did not act or feel as one nation. This is not surprising. In the late 1700s, travel was so slow and difficult that the New England states seemed very far away from the southern states. Today it takes about five hours to drive the 260 miles from Madison's home in Virginia to Philadelphia. When Madison traveled to the Constitutional Convention, it took him twelve days. Besides, cities such as Philadelphia, with its shops, newspapers, paved streets, and brick houses, were a world away from lonely frontier settlements with their mud roads and log cabins. Even the cities along the coast had little contact with each other—they hardly even traded with each other. Most people still made everything they could—cloth and buttons, candles and furniture—at home. The things they had to buy—spices, fine clothing, books, and tea—they bought from England.

A slave market in Charleston, South Carolina

The southern states were still buying African slaves to work on their huge cotton and tobacco plantations. But already slavery divided the nation in half, with the North urging an end to it and the South claiming it couldn't survive without its slaves. At times, it seemed impossible to unite thirteen states that were so far apart and so different. This is the problem that James Madison faced over and over again.

Madison never gave up on the idea of the Union. No matter how many times it looked as if the United States would tear itself apart, he kept trying to hold it together. Madison was a great statesman, but even more important, he was a great thinker. And he had an idea about the United States that kept him fighting for it. How could so many people, so many different people, ever agree?

James Madison appears on this 1809 bronze medal commemorating
a peace treaty between the United States and an Indian tribe.

Madison knew that they never would. But instead of seeing
this as a weakness, Madison regarded it as a strength. With
so many different groups of people, no one group would
ever be able to control all the others. Everyone's freedom
would be safe *because* the country included so many
different opinions.

In 1787 Madison wrote, "The larger the society . . . the
more duly capable it will be of self government." Many
people disagreed with him. They thought a huge republic
like the United States could not last. By the end of
Madison's presidency, in 1817, he could see his words
coming true. The great size and diversity of the United
States were making it strong. That was what James
Madison worked and hoped for his whole life.

Chapter 2

The Education of a Planter's Son

In 1716, Alexander Spotswood, the governor of the colony of Virginia, wanted to find out what lay on the far side of the Blue Ridge Mountains. Spotswood was hoping to find the southern end of Lake Erie. None of the British settlers in Virginia had ever crossed the mountains. Their little towns and farms clung to the coast within reach of British sailing ships. Between the cleared settlements and the mountains was a forest wilderness.

Governor Spotswood hired Indian guides and gathered a small group of men to ride into the wilderness with him. They grandly called themselves the Knights of the Golden Horseshoe. The knights did not find Lake Erie, but along the way they passed what one of them called "the largest timber, the finest and deepest mould [soil], and the best grass I ever did see." The knights looked over the Blue Ridge Mountains and claimed all the land to the west, right up to the Mississippi River, for the King of England and the colony of Virginia. Then they rode home and claimed huge farms in the new lands for themselves.

A Virginia forest

One of the knights, James Taylor II, staked out a 13,500-acre stretch. It was enough land to give each of his children a big estate to clear and farm. One of these estates, a rolling piece of land with a distant view of the Blue Ridge, was to become the lifelong home of Taylor's great-grandson, James Madison.

By the time James Madison was born on March 16, 1751, Taylor's wild forestland had been turned into a busy plantation with acres and acres of tobacco and wheat fields. Trees were cut down and used to build barns, wagons, a flour mill, tobacco-drying sheds, and slaves' cabins.

Throughout Virginia, the hard work of growing tobacco was done by slaves. As a little boy James played with the slave children on his family's plantation. As a man,

16

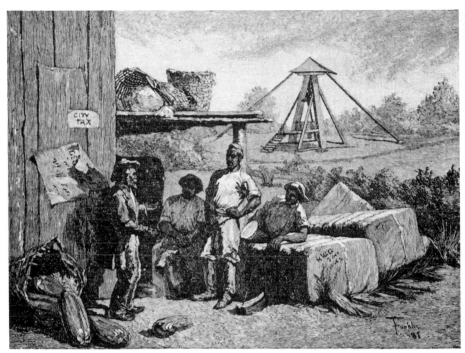
Slaves discussing freedom

Madison believed slavery was wrong, even though his family owned more than one hundred slaves. Madison himself wanted "to depend as little as possible on the labor of slaves." At the same time, he didn't see how the big plantations, including his own, could run without them.

This problem bothered Madison his entire life; he never found a workable solution. He feared that freedom without any other help would not give blacks true equality in a prejudiced white society. Late in his life, Madison was president of a group that resettled freed slaves in Africa. He never sent any of his own slaves back to Africa, though, because the very idea seemed to terrify them. Although Madison always treated his slaves humanely, he did not free them, even in his will.

Far left: A tobacco shop
Above: Lady smoking a pipe
Left: A French snuffbox
for the table

Tobacco was colonial Virginia's most important crop. Throughout Europe, people smoked, chewed, and sniffed it. Grated tobacco for sniffing was called snuff. Many men, and even some women, carried beautifully decorated little snuffboxes with them. (Madison's wife, Dolley, had her own snuffbox and took a pinch now and then.) Virginia landowners, such as the Madisons, sent tobacco to England by the shipload.

As their plantation grew, James's parents could afford to build a new, bigger house. They needed one—by 1760 the Madisons had five children. The new brick house was completed in about 1761. Young James, the oldest child, helped the family move, carrying pieces of furniture the half mile from the old wooden house. The Madisons named the new house Montpelier. Although Madison later held office in many cities, he always thought of Montpelier as his home.

MONTPELIER.

When he was eleven, James went away to school. A Scotsman named Donald Robertson ran the school and taught Latin, Greek, algebra, and logic. Robertson also taught French, but he pronounced it with a Scottish accent. Madison never knew how funny his French sounded until he tried to talk with a Frenchman years later. Still, Robertson was a good teacher. "All that I have been in life I owe largely to that man," Madison wrote.

James stayed at Robertson's school until 1767. Then Madison's father hired Thomas Martin, the new rector of the nearby church, to teach all the younger Madisons and to help James prepare for college. After two years of tutoring at home, James decided to go to the college Martin had attended, the College of New Jersey at Princeton.

That was a surprising choice. New Jersey was a long, hard journey north, and many southern colonists felt uncomfortable among northerners. Most Virginians who went to college attended William and Mary College in Williamsburg, Virginia.

Princeton College, New Jersey

But it was a lucky choice for Madison. The president of Princeton—another Scot, John Witherspoon—was bringing new life to the school. He added about five hundred books to the school's library—a large number for the time—and he encouraged the students to read widely. Students often had to join in debates and deliver speeches. All of this was great training for a future politician. The constant practice in writing clearly about complicated ideas would help Madison all his life.

As a young man, Madison was shy. He had a weak voice and the kind of calm, even personality that didn't go with making fiery or flowery speeches. Later in life when he became used to public speaking, it still suited him to follow Witherspoon's two rules: "Lads, ne'er do ye speak unless ye ha' something to say, and when ye are done, be sure and leave off."

Above: James Madison as a young man
Right: Philip Freneau, poet and novelist

Princeton students worked long days. The morning bell rang to wake them at 5:00 A.M. The students lived three to a room in the college building, Nassau Hall. They worked hard and had only two hours to themselves each day—though they still found time for pranks, such as spreading slippery, greasy feathers in dark doorways. James Madison worked harder than most—he finished college in just two years. But still he had time to join in the poetry wars raging through the school. Around graduation time, Madison and two far better poets, Philip Freneau (later a well-known poet) and Hugh Henry Brackenridge (later a novelist), wrote funny, insulting poems about the members of a rival club.

The highlight of Madison's graduation in 1771 was the reading of another poem by Freneau and Brackenridge, this one a serious, patriotic piece called "The Rising Glory of America." A new feeling of patriotism was rising, not only at Princeton, but all over the colonies. Anger at England was pulling the thirteen colonies together.

Colonial tobacco merchants shipped much of their product to England.

During Madison's college years, England started charging taxes on English products, such as tea and cloth, that the colonists needed. The colonists were caught: they couldn't raise the prices of the flour and fish and lumber and tobacco they sold to the mother country; those prices were set in England. On the other hand, prices for the goods they *bought* from England kept going up and up. The only way the colonists could fight back was to boycott English goods—that is, to refuse to buy them.

Students at Princeton supported the boycott. In 1770, all the graduating seniors wore clothes made of coarse, homespun cloth instead of fine English broadcloth. As one speaker said, the boycott was "a noble Exertion of Self-denial and public Spirit."

The same public spirit was spreading through Virginia when Madison went home in 1772. By 1774, Madison and his father were part of a committee to make sure that no one broke the boycott. In 1775, war broke out between England and the colonies.

Madison himself never fought in the American Revolution. He joined the militia—the local reserve army—and

The young
James Madison
in uniform

practiced with his rifle, but he had an illness that kept him out of battle. One relative wrote that he had sudden attacks of something like epilepsy. Friends thought he had pushed himself too hard at school—indeed, a friend who also finished two years in one had already died. But whatever the cause, Madison recovered very slowly. At twenty-four, he didn't expect to live a long life.

By the time war began, he was feeling better, thanks to "more activity and less study." The English governor of Virginia, Lord Dunmore, fled to a warship in Norfolk Harbor. On New Year's Day of 1776, Governor Dunmore sent troops to burn the city. This fire convinced most Virginians that they no longer needed the mother country. All over the colony, the people picked delegates to set up a new state government independent of England. Orange County, where the Madisons lived, sent two delegates riding through the rain and mud to the convention—William Moore and his nephew James Madison.

Chapter 3

Freedom of Religion

When Madison rode off to the Virginia convention, he didn't know that he had found his life's work. Madison spent the next forty years in public life. He held many different offices, including that of president of the United States. But no one looking around the Virginia convention would have picked Madison as a future president. Indeed, it was easy to overlook him! He was one of the youngest delegates. In a crowd of rangy Virginians, he was also one of the smallest—about five feet, six inches tall. Moreover, because his voice was low and because he was shy, Madison did not make a single speech at the convention. When it came time for him to run for reelection as a delegate, Madison lost, mostly because he refused to give free whiskey to the voters as his opponent did. Madison had a great deal to learn about political life. Beginning with this convention, he learned it very fast.

George Mason of Virginia refused to sign the final draft of the Constitution, partly because it did not include a bill of rights. Many public offices were offered to Mason in his lifetime, but he refused to accept any of them.

Madison listened carefully to the more experienced men, such as the brilliant political thinker George Mason and the great speaker Patrick Henry. The final plan for Virginia's new state government was written mostly by George Mason. Because Virginians wanted to make certain they had a say in their government, the plan called for a strong legislature. The idea was that legislators would listen to the people, because they depended on the people for votes.

And because the colonists hated kings, they were afraid to give any one person too much power. Therefore the governor of the state had very little power. In all official matters he had to get the approval of a council of eight men. Later on, Madison came to see that the governor was too weak to get anything done. For the moment, though, he approved of Mason's plan—except for one sentence.

Mason had written that the state should allow "the fullest toleration in . . . religion." Toleration, however, is not the same thing as freedom. At the time, most Virginians were Anglicans, and the Anglican church was the official religion of Virginia. That meant, among other things, that all taxpayers had to support the Anglican church, whether they were members or not. It meant that people could belong to other religions, but they would still have to contribute to the state's official church.

Madison thought that naming an official church was "making laws for the human mind." He didn't like the idea of a state paying money to one particular church. More important, he felt members of other religions would never be free of prejudice and persecution if there were a state religion. In Orange County, he had already seen Baptists sent to jail for trying to spread their beliefs.

Madison decided to try to change that single sentence of Mason's proposal. It was the beginning of his education in practical politics.

First he wrote out a new version that made two points: (1) all men had an equal right to follow their conscience and (2) there should be no state religion. The convention wasn't ready to abolish the idea of a state religion; it voted against Madison. Then Madison went to Edmund Pendleton, an older delegate and family friend, for help. Pendleton helped Madison rewrite his idea and then read it to the other delegates. This time Madison's change was accepted. The final version says, "All men are equally entitled to the free exercise of religion." Within the year, the legislature did away with the church tax.

Madison had to fight the church tax again eight years later. When he was a member of the Virginia legislature, the Anglican and Presbyterian churches proposed a new kind of church tax. This time there would be no official church; the money would be divided among all the religions in the state.

Patrick Henry was a powerful public speaker whose words roused his fellow citizens to revolt against England. As a member of the Virginia legislature, he spoke out against the Stamp Act of 1765, saying, "If this be treason, make the most of it." In 1775, urging Virginia to take up arms against England, he delivered his most famous words: "Give me liberty or give me death."

The biggest defender of the new tax was none other than Patrick Henry. The great orator gave rousing speeches in favor of the law. Madison thought his own arguments were better than Henry's, but that didn't mean he could beat Henry when the tax came to a vote. He looked for a way to eliminate his opponent.

Working behind the scenes, Madison had Patrick Henry nominated for governor. The office was an honor, but in Virginia it had almost no power. Henry's friends voted for him out of respect. His enemies voted for him to get him out of the way. Henry won and became governor of Virginia. Madison won, too. He won some time to get his ideas past the legislature without worrying about Patrick Henry and his speeches.

Madison thought the common people of Virginia were against the church tax. To prove this he wrote a petition.

The churchyard of Christ Church in Alexandria, Virginia

In it he argued that the government has no right to meddle in religious belief. "The rulers who are guilty of such an encroachment . . . are tyrants. The people who submit to it . . . are slaves." Hundreds of people all over the state signed Madison's petition. In fact, so many people were against the tax that it never even came up for a vote. No one in the legislature ever mentioned it again. Instead, Madison got the legislature to pass a Bill for Religious Liberty, written by Thomas Jefferson.

In the eight years since Madison had joined the Virginia convention, he had learned how to fight a political battle. As a shy, young delegate Madison had been intelligent, well educated, idealistic, and patriotic. He was still all of these things. But now he was also widely respected as a shrewd and flexible statesman. He had won that respect by struggling with one of the hardest problems facing the new country: How should the United States pay its bills?

Continental currency—
Right: This $3 bill shows
an eagle (England)
attacking a weaker bird, the
crane (America). The Latin
motto around the picture
means "The end is in
doubt." This is a warning
that the outcome of the
revolution is uncertain.
Below: The front and back
sides of a one-third-dollar
bill. Benjamin Franklin
suggested the designs. The
motto around the sundial,
"Fugio" ("I fly"), tells the
colonists that time is flying
in their struggle against
England. The linked rings
represent the thirteen
united colonies.

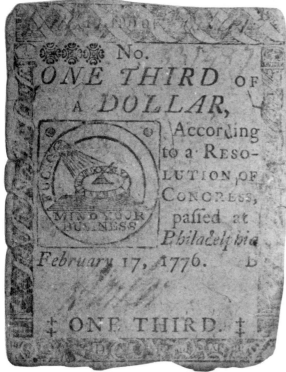

Chapter 4

Paying for the Revolution

In the middle of the revolutionary war, George Washington warned the Continental Congress that his army would "starve, dissolve or disperse." There was no famine in the country; the only people without food were the nation's soldiers. The problem was inflation.

The army paid for its food and supplies with paper money printed by the Continental Congress. But paper money is only valuable when people believe the government can back it up, and people had their doubts about the Continental Congress. Farmers didn't want to be paid with the paper money because they weren't sure they would be able to buy anything with it. Many people simply refused to accept the paper bills, and anyone who did was sure to charge outrageously high prices.

For a while, Congress told the states to send supplies for the army instead of money. In 1778, every county was to send "one pair of Shoes, Stockings, Gloves or Mittens" for every soldier from that county. Then the Continental Congress asked for food. But it was so difficult to move supplies from the states to the army that most of the food rotted in warehouses. The army didn't get a bite of it. Meanwhile the government waited for money from the states, but it never came.

Perhaps the Continental Congress was to blame. Washington pleaded with the states to send "your ablest and best men to Congress." Virginia voted to send James Madison.

As soon as he arrived in Philadelphia for the Congress, Madison learned how serious the money problem was. His room and board for the first six months cost about $2.00 a day in Spanish coins, but in Congress's paper money the bill came to $21,372!

Madison and others in Congress could see that the United States needed money for its army. For the moment the best answer was to borrow money from France. Many Americans didn't want to be in debt to a nation ruled by a king as England and France were. But France was the only country willing to help the United States against England.

In 1781, Congress decided to raise money by charging a small tax or duty on all imports. Whenever an American bought something from another country, Congress would charge a tax of five cents for every dollar it cost. This doesn't seem like very much to ask until you remember that import taxes started the revolutionary war in the first place. There was an important difference, however. England had never asked the colonies to *agree* to pay taxes. The Continental Congress had to get every state's consent.

Wealthy Robert Morris of Pennsylvania was in charge of keeping the United States from going broke. He had gone to extraordinary lengths to do it — sometimes he borrowed money in his own name to meet the government's expenses. But he couldn't borrow money forever without any tax money coming in from the states. He wrote an

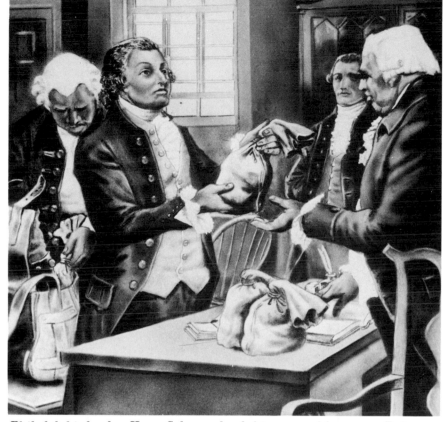

Philadelphia banker Haym Salomon lends his personal fortune to Robert Morris to support the revolution. Salomon died penniless. The government never repaid to him or his heirs the estimated $660,000 it owed.

angry letter threatening the states. If the army fell apart, he wrote, "the fault is in the states; they have been deaf to the calls of Congress, to the clamors of the public creditors, to the just demands of a suffering army, and even to the reproaches of the enemy, who scoffingly declare that the army is fed, paid and clothed by France."

All Morris's accusations were true. But Madison didn't let him send the letter. It would have made all the state governors angry enough to vote against the tax. Instead, Madison proposed sending delegates to every state to describe how desperate the need was. This plan almost worked. Every state except the tiniest one, Rhode Island, agreed to the import duty.

Rhode Island's delegates argued that they wanted to give Congress money "like freemen, from time to time, bound only . . . by your sacred honor." In fact, Rhode Island's freemen didn't want to give any money at all, but their argument was hard to answer. The states wanted to keep control of taxes. They wanted to use state money to pay state citizens and state expenses.

Madison and the Congress disagreed. If the United States borrowed money as a country, it should repay it as a country. If one state were attacked, all the others should help pay for its defense. Meanwhile, the Congress had no money. The army was ready to revolt. To keep going, Congress had to borrow more from France. But how long would France lend money when the United States seemed to have no way of repaying it?

When the people of Virginia heard about the "perverse sister," Rhode Island, they changed their vote. So now Virginia opposed the import tax, too, and sent instructions to its delegates in Congress: all Virginia delegates must vote against the import tax.

Madison had to decide whether to follow his state's orders or his conscience. He stood up to argue his case. First, he said, each delegate had a duty, not only to his own state, but also to the country as a whole. Only a federal tax controlled by the Congress could pay all the country's bills fairly. The only other choice was not to repay France and not to support the American soldiers.

"The idea of erecting our national independence on the ruins of public faith and national honor must be horrid to every mind which retained either honesty or pride," he told his fellow delegates. Madison followed his conscience; he voted for a federal import tax.

Then Madison had an idea—why not combine the tax plan with things that individual states wanted? Why not give the states a good reason for voting "yes" on the tax? Congress agreed to try it and asked Madison to write the new proposal. Madison worked on it for two days. He took the import duty proposal and added "bait" for the states. For example, the bill proposed that the federal government help repair the damage done by the British army. This was good bait for Virginia, New York, Georgia, and the Carolinas.

Combining proposals to get votes in this way is called "logrolling." Today it is a well-known strategy. But this was the first logrolling bill in U.S. history. Congress passed the bill, but it still needed the states' approval.

In June 1783, England gave up and offered to make peace. Independence was won—the war was over. Without the fear of war, it became even less likely that the states would act together for the common good.

Madison's term in Congress ended in October 1783. The following year Orange County sent him back to the Virginia legislature. Now he had a chance to fight for Virginia's vote on the federal tax bill. Patrick Henry was on his side at first. The tax bill passed. Then Madison suggested that Virginia begin by paying its back taxes—the state hadn't paid Congress any money for three years.

To Madison, it seemed like a good year to start paying. With the peace, tobacco prices were very high. For the moment, the Virginia planters had a lot of money. But

Patrick Henry stood in Madison's way. Even though the state was very prosperous, Henry wanted to postpone all tax payments for another year. Madison knew that if Virginia, the largest state, failed to pay, the jealous small states would also hold back their money. Madison was right, but there was no stopping Patrick Henry. The postponement passed.

Madison watched what happened in the other states. Amazingly, Rhode Island passed the tax proposal. But Connecticut, New Jersey, and Delaware declared that they would not collect the tax in their ports. They did this to draw business away from the Massachusetts, Pennsylvania, and New York ports that were collecting the tax. Nothing could possibly look worse than America's federal affairs, wrote Madison. "No money comes into the public treasury, trade is on a wretched footing. . . ."

In 1786, Virginia sent Madison to a meeting that was supposed to solve trade squabbles among the states. By this time, the states couldn't agree even to discuss their problems. Only five states sent representatives. The few delegates started talking about all the problems that were tearing the new country apart. They ended up calling for a national convention in May 1787 where the states would discuss not just trade, but the whole government of the United States.

Persuading the states to agree to this new convention looked like an impossible job. But a farmers' uprising in Massachusetts, called Shays's Rebellion, scared all thirteen states. The Continental Congress was unable to help Massachusetts. It became obvious to everyone that the

A mob scene in Springfield, Massachusetts, during Shays's Rebellion

Congress couldn't govern the states; it was too clumsy, too slow, too weak, and worst of all, completely broke. The states voted in favor of the new convention. Virginia approved the idea unanimously. Madison was relieved.

This convention offered the states another chance. Madison had a feeling it would be their last. Maybe this time they would come up with a strong, workable government. If not, he said, the thirteen states "pulling against each other . . . will soon bring ruin on the whole."

The adoption of the U.S. Constitution on September 17, 1787.
James Madison is seated third from the left.

Chapter 5

The Constitutional Convention

Struggles in the Continental Congress showed Madison that the Union needed a strong national government. But how could the country have a strong government without taking away the people's freedom?

To answer this question, Madison read trunkloads of books about government and history. Centuries before the thirteen states banded together, the ancient Greeks had tried the same thing. Centuries before the Americans founded a republic, the Romans had tried it. Madison studied these governments carefully. How were they put together? Why did they fall apart? How could the American states succeed where the Greeks and the Romans had failed?

By the end of his winter's reading, Madison had a plan. First he convinced his own state's delegates, including national hero George Washington and Virginia governor Edmund Randolph, to back his plan. The Constitutional Convention opened on May 25, 1787. It would not finish until September 17. In the first week, Washington was elected convention president and Randolph read Madison's plan, called the Virginia Plan, to the assembly.

Madison had two goals in writing his plan. First, he wanted to make the central government much stronger than it had been under the Articles of Confederation—strong enough to force the states to pay their taxes, strong enough to earn the respect of foreign countries. But the states had just fought a long, hard revolution to free themselves from a strong government that paid no attention to their wishes. Madison wanted to design a government that couldn't become *too* strong.

Madison's plan was to divide the central government into three branches: a legislative branch to make laws, an executive branch to carry them out, and a judicial branch to settle disputes about what those laws mean. The legislature would also be divided into two groups or houses, a House of Representatives and a Senate. The strength of the national government would come, not from a large army or from harsh laws, but from the consent of the people. The Virginia Plan called for a republic where the people would vote directly for their representatives.

The convention easily accepted the idea of a three-branched national government with a two-house legislature. Then came a big clash over the office of president. Some of the delegates, led by Randolph of Virginia, were afraid of giving one man so much power. What would keep him from becoming a greedy tyrant? To these delegates, a "president" sounded like a "king" and the states had just gotten rid of a king!

On the other side, many delegates, especially those from New England, were just as afraid of giving much power to the people. After Shays's Rebellion, many of these

Left: Edmund Randolph. Right: James Wilson

men had lost faith in the people's intelligence and good will. Elbridge Gerry of Massachusetts said the states already had an "excess of democracy." Alexander Hamilton of New York even proposed that the president hold office for life, making him very much like a king!

Madison and James Wilson of Pennsylvania took turns reassuring both sides. Wilson was a tall, heavy man who wore the thick glasses of a serious reader. He knew the history of governments inside out. Wilson insisted that a strong government must win the support of "the people at large." Madison reassured the worried delegates that a government could be both strong and free.

After their speeches, the delegates agreed to accept the office of president. Without saying a word, George Washington helped sway the vote. Everyone expected that Washington would be the first president. No one could imagine him ruling like a tyrant or a weakling.

To all to whom

these Presents shall come, we the undersigned Delegates of the States
affixed to our Names send greeting. Whereas the Delegates of the
United States of America in Congress assembled did on the fifteenth day
of November in the Year of our Lord One Thousand Seven Hundred and
Seventy seven, and in the Second Year of the Independence of America
agree to certain articles of Confederation and perpetual Union between the
States of New hampshire, Massachusetts-bay, Rhode island and Providence
Plantations, Connecticut, New York, New Jersey, Pennsylvania, Delaware,
Maryland, Virginia, North Carolina, South Carolina and Georgia
in the Words following, viz. "Articles of Confederation and perpetual
Union between the States of Newhampshire, Massachusetts-bay, Rhode island
and Providence Plantations, Connecticut, New York, New Jersey, Pennsylvania, Delaware, Maryland, Virginia, North Carolina, South Carolina
and Georgia.

Article 1. The Stile of this confederacy shall be "The
United States of America".

Article II. Each state retains its sovereignty, freedom and
independence, and every Power, Jurisdiction and right, which is not by
this confederation expressly delegated to the United States, in Congress
assembled.

Article III. The said states hereby severally enter into a firm
league of friendship with each other, for their common defence, the security
of their Liberties, and their mutual and general welfare, binding themselves to assist each other, against all force offered to, or attacks made upon
them, or any of them on account of religion, sovereignty, trade, or any other
pretence whatever.

Article IV. The better to secure and perpetuate mutual friendship
and intercourse among the people of the different states in this union, the
free inhabitants of each of these states, paupers, vagabonds and fugitives
from Justice excepted shall be entitled to all privileges and immunities of
free citizens in the several states; and the people of each state shall have
free ingress and regress to and from any other state, and shall enjoy therein
all the privileges of trade and commerce, subject to the same duties, impo-
sitions and restrictions as the inhabitants thereof respectively, provided

The delegates also agreed to have the people elect members of the House of Representatives directly. But this decision led to the longest battle of the convention. Under the old Articles of Confederation, each state had had one vote in the Continental Congress. No matter how big or small, each state had equal power. In a republic, this would have to change. States would have votes according to how many people lived in each state. That meant the big states, such as Virginia and Pennsylvania, would have many more votes than the small ones, such as Delaware and New Jersey. This one idea caused weeks of fighting.

William Paterson stormed that New Jersey would never join any Union only to be "swallowed up!" Angry James Wilson argued back, "If the small States will not confederate on this plan, Pennsylvania . . . would not confederate on any other. . . . If New Jersey will not part with her Sovereignty, it is in vain to talk of Government."

Benjamin Franklin, too old and ill to stand and read his own speeches, tried to calm the angry delegates. Wilson read his speech for him: "We are sent here to consult, not to contend, with each other and declarations of a fixed opinion, and of determined resolution, never to change it, neither enlighten nor convince us."

Unfortunately, neither side took Franklin's warning to heart. As the summer became hotter, opinions hardened on both sides. Paterson came up with the outrageous New Jersey Plan, proposing to chop up all the states into equal-sized chunks. Madison defeated Paterson's plan by pointing out that the small states needed the protection of a strong national government more than the large states did.

Opposite: The Articles of Confederation

43

But the fight still wasn't over. Day after baking day the delegates argued back and forth, the same arguments over and over, and neither side would back down. On one of the hotter days of the long summer, fat, uncomfortable Gunning Bedford of Delaware upset everyone by yelling at the big-state delegates, "I do not, gentlemen, trust you!"

Bedford answered Madison's argument with a terrible threat: The small states didn't need the Union because they could always get the help of foreign countries. In other words, the small states would rather abandon the Union and join with England unless they had power equal to the large states.

Without some compromise, the convention was ready to break apart.

The compromise came from Roger Sherman of Connecticut. Why not give each state votes in the House according to state population, while giving each state the same number of votes in the Senate? The great compromise gave each group half of what it wanted. No one was sure if enough states would be satisfied with that.

Each state at the convention had one vote, but not all the states had delegates there all the time. New Hampshire's delegates were more than a month late; New York's delegates had already walked out; Rhode Island never sent anyone. The Massachusetts delegates couldn't agree on this issue, so they cast no vote. Madison was against the compromise—he and Wilson led Virginia, Pennsylvania, South Carolina, and Georgia in voting no. But five states—Connecticut, New Jersey, Delaware, Maryland, and North Carolina—voted yes.

Opposite: The beginning of the U.S. Constitution

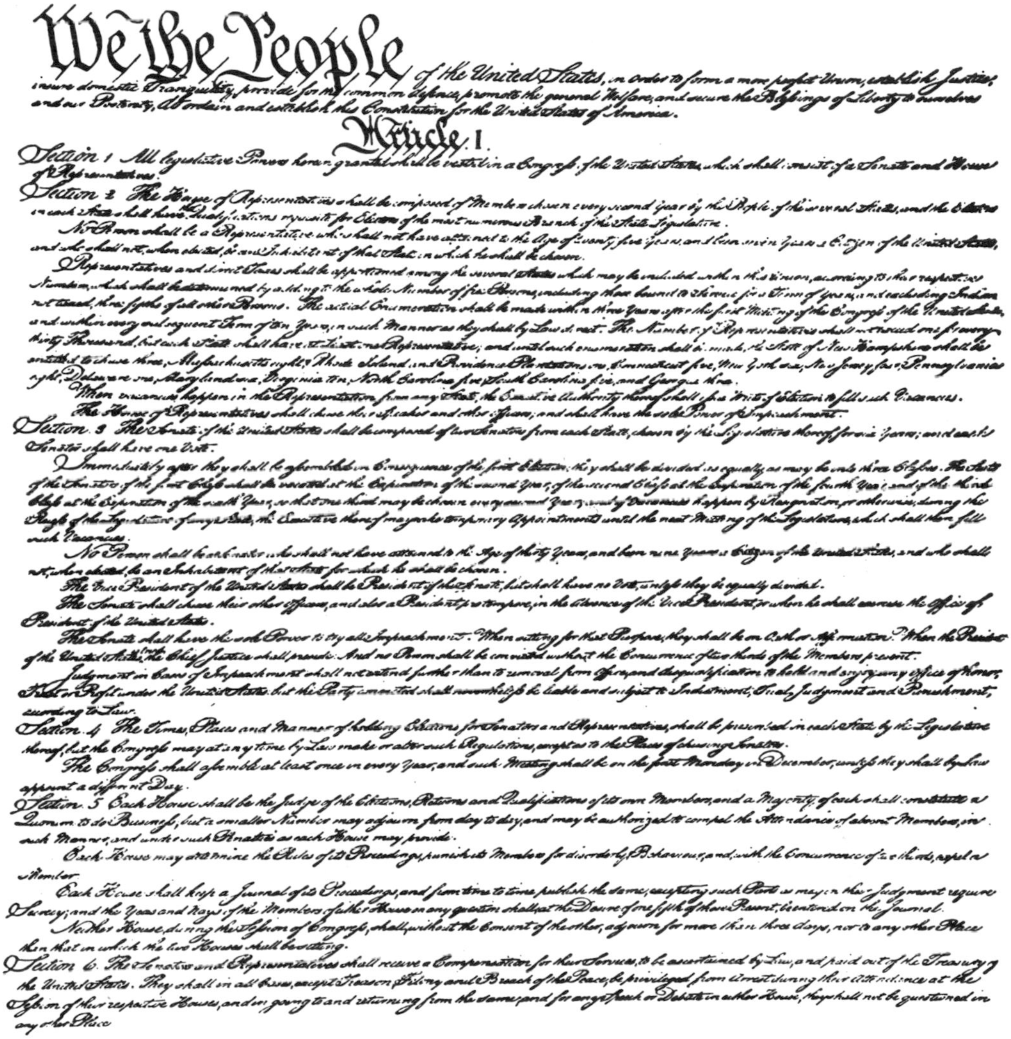
We the People of the United States, in Order to form a more perfect Union, establish Justice, insure domestic Tranquility, provide for the common defence, promote the general Welfare, and secure the Blessings of Liberty to ourselves and our Posterity, do ordain and establish this Constitution for the United States of America.

Article. I.

Section. 1. All legislative Powers herein granted shall be vested in a Congress of the United States, which shall consist of a Senate and House of Representatives.

Section. 2. The House of Representatives shall be composed of Members chosen every second Year by the People of the several States, and the Electors in each State shall have the Qualifications requisite for Electors of the most numerous Branch of the State Legislature.

No Person shall be a Representative who shall not have attained to the Age of twenty five Years, and been seven Years a Citizen of the United States, and who shall not, when elected, be an Inhabitant of that State in which he shall be chosen.

Representatives and direct Taxes shall be apportioned among the several States which may be included within this Union, according to their respective Numbers, which shall be determined by adding to the whole Number of free Persons, including those bound to Service for a Term of Years, and excluding Indians not taxed, three fifths of all other Persons. The actual Enumeration shall be made within three Years after the first Meeting of the Congress of the United States, and within every subsequent Term of ten Years, in such Manner as they shall by Law direct. The Number of Representatives shall not exceed one for every thirty Thousand, but each State shall have at Least one Representative; and until such enumeration shall be made, the State of New Hampshire shall be entitled to chuse three, Massachusetts eight, Rhode Island and Providence Plantations one, Connecticut five, New York six, New Jersey four, Pennsylvania eight, Delaware one, Maryland six, Virginia ten, North Carolina five, South Carolina five, and Georgia three.

When vacancies happen in the Representation from any State, the Executive Authority thereof shall issue Writs of Election to fill such Vacancies.

The House of Representatives shall chuse their Speaker and other Officers; and shall have the sole Power of Impeachment.

Section. 3. The Senate of the United States shall be composed of two Senators from each State, chosen by the Legislature thereof for six Years; and each Senator shall have one Vote.

Immediately after they shall be assembled in Consequence of the first Election, they shall be divided as equally as may be into three Classes. The Seats of the Senators of the first Class shall be vacated at the Expiration of the second Year, of the second Class at the Expiration of the fourth Year, and of the third Class at the Expiration of the sixth Year, so that one third may be chosen every second Year; and if Vacancies happen by Resignation, or otherwise, during the Recess of the Legislature of any State, the Executive thereof may make temporary Appointments until the next Meeting of the Legislature, which shall then fill such Vacancies.

No Person shall be a Senator who shall not have attained to the Age of thirty Years, and been nine Years a Citizen of the United States, and who shall not, when elected, be an Inhabitant of that State for which he shall be chosen.

The Vice President of the United States shall be President of the Senate, but shall have no Vote, unless they be equally divided.

The Senate shall chuse their other Officers, and also a President pro tempore, in the Absence of the Vice President, or when he shall exercise the Office of President of the United States.

The Senate shall have the sole Power to try all Impeachments. When sitting for that Purpose, they shall be on Oath or Affirmation. When the President of the United States is tried, the Chief Justice shall preside: And no Person shall be convicted without the Concurrence of two thirds of the Members present.

Judgment in Cases of Impeachment shall not extend further than to removal from Office, and disqualification to hold and enjoy any Office of honor, Trust or Profit under the United States: but the Party convicted shall nevertheless be liable and subject to Indictment, Trial, Judgment and Punishment, according to Law.

Section. 4. The Times, Places and Manner of holding Elections for Senators and Representatives, shall be prescribed in each State by the Legislature thereof; but the Congress may at any time by Law make or alter such Regulations, except as to the Places of chusing Senators.

The Congress shall assemble at least once in every Year, and such Meeting shall be on the first Monday in December, unless they shall by Law appoint a different Day.

Section. 5. Each House shall be the Judge of the Elections, Returns and Qualifications of its own Members, and a Majority of each shall constitute a Quorum to do Business; but a smaller Number may adjourn from day to day, and may be authorized to compel the Attendance of absent Members, in such Manner, and under such Penalties as each House may provide.

Each House may determine the Rules of its Proceedings, punish its Members for disorderly Behaviour, and, with the Concurrence of two thirds, expel a Member.

Each House shall keep a Journal of its Proceedings, and from time to time publish the same, excepting such Parts as may in their Judgment require Secrecy; and the Yeas and Nays of the Members of either House on any question shall, at the Desire of one fifth of those Present, be entered on the Journal.

Neither House, during the Session of Congress, shall, without the Consent of the other, adjourn for more than three days, nor to any other Place than that in which the two Houses shall be sitting.

Section. 6. The Senators and Representatives shall receive a Compensation for their Services, to be ascertained by Law, and paid out of the Treasury of the United States. They shall in all Cases, except Treason, Felony and Breach of the Peace, be privileged from Arrest during their Attendance at the Session of their respective Houses, and in going to and returning from the same; and for any Speech or Debate in either House, they shall not be questioned in any other Place.

Madison was disappointed, but he did not let his disappointment sour him. He kept working to design a government that would work. All in all, Madison made 161 speeches that summer. He was involved in every detail of the new Constitution. By the end of the summer, the convention had a Constitution that Madison was proud to sign. Later in his life Madison wrote, "The problem to be solved is, not what form of Government is perfect, but which of the forms is least imperfect."

THE

FEDERALIST,

ON THE NEW CONSTITUTION.

BY *PUBLIUS.*

WRITTEN IN 1738.

TO WHICH IS ADDED,

PACIFICUS,

ON THE PROCLAMATION OF NEUTRALITY.

WRITTEN IN 1793.

LIKEWISE,

The Federal Constitution,

WITH ALL THE AMENDMENTS.

———

REVISED AND CORRECTED.

——— ✳ ———

IN TWO VOLUMES.

....

VOL. I.

——— ✳ ———

COPY-RIGHT SECURED.

═══════════════

New-York:

PRINTED AND SOLD BY GEORGE F. HOPKINS,

At Washington's Head.

....

1802.

Chapter 6

Starting Up

James Madison and Alexander Hamilton didn't see eye to eye on many things. Hamilton respected aristocrats; Madison, the common people. But each man admired the other, and they agreed on one important thing—that the new Constitution was much much better than the Articles of Confederation. As soon as the Constitutional Convention ended, Madison and Hamilton teamed up to work on the next step, getting the states to approve, or ratify, the Constitution. Not all the states had to approve—the new government could start as soon as nine of the thirteen states voted for it.

Together with John Jay, Madison and Hamilton wrote eighty-five newspaper articles explaining the new Constitution and answering arguments against it. Madison wrote twenty-nine of these essays; Hamilton, fifty-one; and Jay, five. All the essays were signed with the same pen name, Publius. The whole series of articles, now called *The Federalist*, was the first explanation of the United States Constitution, and it is still one of the best.

Opposite: The cover of *The Federalist*

As Madison worked in New York, states slowly began to ratify. In every state there were people who opposed the Constitution for one reason or another. Worst of all, some of the convention delegates themselves were against the Constitution they had helped to make. Virginia's George Mason claimed he "would sooner chop off his right hand than put it to the Constitution as it now stands."

By spring 1788, eight states had ratified the Constitution. Only one more state's vote was needed. Madison realized that his own state, Virginia, might not accept the Constitution. George Mason was campaigning against it and he had won over Madison's old opponent, Patrick Henry. Together Mason and Henry could sway the state. Madison's friends in Virginia begged him to come home to help win the state's approval.

It was quite a fight. Patrick Henry—tall, commanding, dramatic, and loud—delivered long speeches that worked on people's fears. In his final retort to Madison, Henry said, "The gentleman has told you of the numerous blessings which he imagines will result to us and the world in general from the adoption of this system. I see the awful immensity of the dangers . . . I see it—I feel it. I see beings of a higher order anxious concerning our decision."

Henry was such an inspiring speaker that no one noticed how often he contradicted himself—until Madison began to answer him point by point. As Madison spoke, he swayed back and forth clasping his hat, which was full of notes. He still was not an inspiring speaker, nor a loud one, but he was logical, knowledgeable, clear, and in the end, convincing. Virginia ratified the Constitution, 89 to 79.

Opposite: Article 37 of *The Federalist*, written by James Madison

THE FEDERALIST.

NUMBER XXXVII.

[By James Madison.]

CONCERNING THE DIFFICULTIES WHICH THE CONVEN-
TION MUST HAVE EXPERIENCED IN THE FORMATION
OF A PROPER PLAN.

In reviewing the defects of the existing confederation, and showing that they cannot be supplied by a government of less energy than that before the public, several of the most important principles of the latter fell of course under consideration. But as the ultimate object of these papers is, to determine clearly and fully the merits of this constitution, and the expediency of adopting it, our plan cannot be completed without taking a more critical and thorough survey of the work of the convention; without examining it on all its sides; comparing it in all its parts, and calculating its probable effects.

The Ninth PILLAR erected !

"The Ratification of the Conventions of nine States, shall be sufficient for the establishment of this Constitution, between the States so ratifying the same." *Art.* vii.

INCIPIENT MAGNI PROCEDERE MENSES.

Nine of the thirteen states had to ratify the Constitution before it could go into effect. In this 1788 cartoon, those first nine states are shown as pillars supporting the arches of government. Virginia and New York, the next two pillars, ratified next. Finally, in 1789 and 1790, North Carolina and Rhode Island gave their approval.

By July 1788, ten states—all but New York, North Carolina, and Rhode Island—had ratified. The United States had a new government. Madison made sure he would be part of it. He ran a friendly campaign against his friend James Monroe for a seat in the House of Representatives and won.

On the very first day of the first session of the new Congress, Madison called for a tax on imports. Under the Articles of Confederation, Madison had tried and failed to win state approval for this very tax. Under the Constitution, Congress had the power to approve taxes. The bill passed. At last, the national government had an income.

Many people were still worried about all the government's new powers. They wanted the Constitution also to guarantee the people's rights. Madison had hundreds of suggestions from the state ratifying conventions. He carefully boiled them down into a list of basic rights, including freedom of religion, freedom of the press, and the right to a public trial. Congress voted to add Madison's ten amendments to the Constitution as the Bill of Rights. The new government was off to a good start.

George Washington is sworn in as first president of the United States
in New York City on April 30, 1789. Adams stands next to Washington.

As everyone expected, George Washington was elected
the first president. His inauguration day ended with a big
fireworks display. So many people crowded to see it that
carriages couldn't move through the crowd. Even the new
president had to walk home!

Washington wasn't sure how a president should act, so
he turned for advice to his friend Madison. In Madison's
opinion, "The more simple, the more Republican we are in
our manners, the more rational dignity we shall acquire."
This suited Washington's own natural dignity of character.

For example, Madison wanted to call Washington simply
"the president of the United States." Vice-President John
Adams disagreed. According to Adams, "All the world,
civilized and savage, called for titles." He convinced the
Senate to call Washington "His Highness, the President of
the United States of America, and Protector of the Rights
of the Same."

51

People joked that, since Adams expected to be the next president, he was really choosing a title for himself. A committee was chosen to settle the title fight. Luckily for Washington and all future presidents, Madison won.

The title fight was a light skirmish compared to the battles that marked Madison's eight years in the House. On issue after issue, Congress was divided into two camps. One group, called the Republicans, centered around Madison and his close friend Secretary of State Thomas Jefferson. The other, called the Federalists, centered around Secretary of the Treasury Alexander Hamilton. This was the beginning of the two-party system still in existence today. Madison's Republican party eventually changed its name, becoming today's Democratic party.

These two political parties stood against each other on a whole list of issues. The Federalists were northeasterners; they wanted the capital of the country to be New York City or Philadelphia. The Republicans were mostly southerners and frontierspeople. They wanted the capital to be farther south, on the Potomac River.

Many Federalists were bankers and merchants; keeping close ties with England was good for their business. Many Republicans were farmers; close ties with France would give them a new market. The Federalists favored the wealthy; the Republicans were for the commoners.

At first, the Republicans had the best of it. Congress voted to build a new capital city on the Potomac, as they wanted. But little by little, Washington began to side with Hamilton and the Federalists. Jefferson and Madison found that their Republican party was losing power.

New York City was the nation's capital from 1785 to 1790; Philadelphia, from 1790 to 1800; and Washington, D.C., from 1800 on. Above: In this 1790 cartoon, New Yorkers criticize Federalist banker Robert Morris for the part he played in having the capital moved to Philadelphia. Right: Republicans Thomas Jefferson and James Madison discuss the site of the future capital, later named Washington, D.C.

Above: The room in which the Madisons were married. Opposite: Montpelier

When Federalist John Adams was elected president in 1796, Madison knew he would not be wanted in the new government. He went home. At the time he believed he was retiring for good, after twenty years in public office.

But Madison didn't return to Montpelier alone. On September 15, 1794, he had married a Quaker widow named Dolley Payne Todd. Dolley Madison was a pretty and kindhearted woman, seventeen years younger than Madison. She had black hair and deep blue eyes. The two were exactly the same height. While Madison always wore sedate black clothes, Dolley like big hats, turbans with feathers, and elegant dresses. Madison seemed stiff and cold unless he was with close friends. Dolley was lively and warm and charming to roomfuls of people.

The Madisons were certainly not very much alike, but they were very happy together. On their wedding day, Madison added an embroidered waistcoat and a fine lace neckpiece to his usual black suit. Later he was so happy he let friends cut up his neckpiece for wedding souvenirs.

Together the Madisons went back to Montpelier to farm and wait out the Adams years. By 1800, the people were so unhappy with Adams and the Federalists that they voted Republican. Madison's close friend Thomas Jefferson became president, and he immediately called on Madison to be his secretary of state.

Dolley Madison was famous as a gracious and tactful hostess. She was also known for her fashionable hats and turbans. She was a widow when she married James Madison at the age of 26. After Madison died in 1836, Dolley moved from Montpelier back to Washington, D.C., where she lived until her death at age 81.

Washington, D.C., was a raw, unfinished town when the Madisons moved
there in 1801. The British burned the city, including the White House,
during the War of 1812, but it was soon rebuilt. This picture shows a view of
the new White House across the Potomac River around 1820.

Chapter 7

Secretary of State

When the Madisons arrived in Washington in 1801, all they saw were a few buildings connected by mud roads. There were not many houses. The Capitol building was only half-finished. The White House stood in the middle of a field. Inside, it was still full of carpenters and damp plaster. The only place to go for fun was the racetrack, where, in the fall, everybody stood on refreshment tables or sat in carriages to watch the races.

To this raw, half-built city came ministers from England, France, and Spain. As secretary of state, Madison had to entertain these diplomats as well as negotiate with them. At one of the Madisons' receptions, a group of American Indians had a disagreement over religion with Sidi Suliman Mellimelli, a Tunisian envoy wearing a huge white turban made from twenty yards of cloth. On another evening, Madison had to stop a loud, scandalous fight between the French minister and his wife.

The English minister was upset because President Jefferson wore old clothes and slippers to their first meeting. He was even angrier because his wife didn't get to sit beside the president at a dinner party. This social disagreement made it harder for Madison to work with the English minister on the more serious disagreements between the two nations.

Across the ocean, England was at war with France. The French ruler, Napoleon, was trying to conquer all of Europe. He was winning on land, but with the world's best navy, Great Britain controlled the seas. Madison and Jefferson wanted to keep America out of this war. Staying neutral wasn't easy. At home, the Federalists wanted to declare war on France; the Republicans wanted to declare war on England. However, neutrality won two big gains for the United States.

First, Napoleon knew he couldn't fight in Europe and hold on to land in America at the same time. With constant pressure from Madison, he sold the entire Louisiana Territory to the United States for only $15 million. Republicans were overjoyed to add this huge piece of land to the United States. The Louisiana Territory stretched from the Gulf of Mexico north to Minnesota and from the Mississippi west to the Rocky Mountains.

The Federalists were furious; they complained about spending all that money to buy what they called a desert. They didn't want their eastern states to be outnumbered by a host of new states. One Federalist congressman poked fun at the raw congressmen he expected would come from the new territory: "Thick-skinned beasts will crowd Con-

The Louisiana Purchase doubled the size of the United States.

gress Hall—buffaloes from the head of the Missouri and alligators from the Red River." In spite of the Federalists' complaints, the Louisiana Purchase was a great triumph for Jefferson and his secretary of state.

Americans were also gaining tremendously from increased wartime trade. Since it was neutral, the United States could do business with both England and France. For manufacturers, farmers, and shippers, business was booming—that is, until American prosperity began to bother Great Britain.

The British government proclaimed what they called the Orders in Council—no neutral ships were allowed to trade with France unless they first bought a special license in Great Britain. When he heard about the British Orders, Napoleon ordered French warships to capture every ship going to or from Great Britain. American traders were in a bind. If they tried to trade with either country, the other would capture their ships, take the cargo, and, frequently, burn the ships.

Impressment—forcing American seamen aboard British ships—was one of Madison's problems as secretary of state.

On top of all this, when British captains needed more sailors, they took men from American crews by force. The British called this impressment. They defended it by claiming that the impressed men were British deserters. Madison checked. In four years, only two out of 2,059 impressed seamen were really British citizens.

In spite of protests from Madison, British sea captains grew bolder and bolder. In June 1807, the British ship *Leopard* actually followed the American ship *Chesapeake* out to sea, demanded three crewmen, then opened fire, blasting twenty-two holes in the *Chesapeake*. Three American sailors were killed and eighteen wounded. The *Leopard* sailed away with four men from the *Chesapeake*.

Rather than start a costly war, Jefferson called for an embargo, a halt to American trade with Europe. He asked Congress, "If therefore on leaving our harbors we are certain to lose them, is it not better as to vessels, cargoes and seamen to keep them at home?" Congress agreed.

The embargo passed but it didn't work. Merchants and farmers were losing money. Many of the New England states cheated by smuggling goods out to England. Although Madison won the Republican nomination for president in 1808, the people's anger over the embargo almost cost him the election.

His own Republican party divided against Madison to back his friend and fellow Virginian, James Monroe. Monroe had just come home from England where Jefferson had sent him to work on a treaty. Jefferson and Madison rejected Monroe's treaty because it said nothing about their two major complaints, impressment and the Orders in Council. Federalist newspapers claimed Madison wouldn't make peace with England because he was taking bribes from Napoleon. The only way to expose such lies was to let the whole country read Madison's state papers. His letters to Monroe showed that Madison gave England every chance to stop impressment without ever backing down on America's rights.

Reading Madison's letters turned public opinion in his favor. One usually anti-Madison newspaperman wrote, "The man who can read this able and spirited paper without feeling his pride increased and his indignation excited, ought to suspect his head of imbecility, and his heart of insensibility to virtue or patriotism."

Soon Monroe dropped out of the race for president. In November 1808, Madison won the election with 122 electoral votes to Federalist Charles Pinckney's 47. On March 4, 1809, James Madison became the fourth president of the United States.

A view of Washington, D.C., in 1810, when James Madison was president

Chapter 8

First Term

So many people crowded into Madison's inaugural ball that guests broke the ballroom windows to get fresh air. When the celebration was over, Madison faced a very difficult situation. Although the Federalists had been weak all through Jefferson's presidency, the embargo gave them an issue to attack. Now the reawakened Federalists stood ready to oppose and criticize every step Madison took.

The three presidents before Madison usually had been able to count on support from Congress, but in 1808 Congress was divided, too. Republicans controlled the House of Representatives, but one Republican leader, John Randolph, hated Madison and worked against him. In the Senate, three power-hungry senators led by Samuel Smith of Maryland often swung victory to the Federalists.

The American people were tired of losing money on the embargo. They wanted war but couldn't agree on which country to fight first, France or England. Congress was against war altogether because it didn't want to raise taxes for building ships and paying an army. Instead of the embargo, which kept American goods at home, Congress passed a nonimportation bill. This meant that the U.S. refused to buy anything from England or France.

American merchant vessels near Crowninshield's Wharf in Salem, Massachusetts

Meanwhile both England and France kept up their attacks on neutral American ships. Napoleon needed the money he made selling American cargoes. England, as Madison realized, simply didn't want any trade competition from America. The purpose of the English blockade of French ports was not to cut off supplies. England let her own merchants sell to France! The purpose was to keep all the European trade for England.

Both England and France were doing their best to drag the U.S. into the war. Madison decided to use this very threat against both countries. He promised both Great Britain and France that if one of them would stop harassing American ships, the U.S. would make war on the other one. In exchange for allowing America to trade freely, either country could have an ally in its war.

Madison sent this message two weeks after he became president. He didn't want to fight unless there was no peaceful way to protect American trade. If the U.S. had to fight, he wanted to make sure it would take on only one enemy at a time. His strategy worked, but it took four long years before one of the European countries gave way on neutral trading. What took so long?

Madison was working under three handicaps: his secretary of state, Robert Smith, was a blunderer; the Federalist party didn't like Madison and wanted to preserve trade with England; and, finally, communications across the Atlantic were terribly slow.

Madison appointed Smith as secretary of state hoping to win the support of Smith's brother, the powerful Maryland senator Samuel Smith. But Robert Smith proved to be so unreliable and so indiscreet that Madison ended up writing all Smith's letters for him. To the French minister, Smith was pleasantly pro-French, to the British minister, pleasantly pro-British. To both he portrayed Madison as "perhaps too timid," so that neither believed Madison when he threatened war. Finally, Madison dismissed Smith and named James Monroe secretary of state.

Long misled by Smith, the French minister Louis Sérurier began to realize that Madison had "some toughness of character when he thinks the national honor is involved." The French government was the first to budge. In 1810, France promised to lift its restrictions against American trade. Napoleon was slow to keep that promise. Sérurier kept warning his government that Madison was serious when he said he would go to war. He urged his country to live up to its word. In July 1811, France released all captured American ships. Madison was now free to act against England.

Right up to the very eve of war, the British didn't believe the United States would fight. Rather than believe Madison or Monroe, the British minister Augustus Foster relied on the opinions of his American friends, the Federalists. The New England Federalists had always been pro-British; now Federalist congressmen told Foster that half the country (their half) would never vote for war. When the Senate cut the army's budget from $3 million to $1 million, it convinced Foster that his Federalist friends were right.

The French minister Sérurier realized that Madison was "thwarted by the eternal censure of newspapers and the clamor of parties." Foster didn't seem to realize that he was in the middle of party politics; what the Federalists told him, he took at face value. Worse, it was only the Federalists' opinions (for example, that Madison was "too weak to be wicked") that he reported. Only months before war broke out, he wrote, "There never was a more favorable moment for Great Britain to impose almost what terms she pleases upon the United States."

By then, Great Britain held 6,200 American seamen and refused to stop impressment. In April 1812, Madison called for an embargo in order to get all American ships home before declaring war. Acquaintances began to ask Foster if they could buy his horses when he left the country. To his government, Foster wrote that it was all election-year politics.

This 1813 British cartoon shows an American seaman (the skeleton) and a British seaman exchanging threats and insults during the War of 1812.

Madison actually started preparing the country for war in November 1811. But he didn't want to declare war without giving Great Britain one last chance. He waited for the British ship *Hornet* to bring the latest packet of letters from the English government. The *Hornet* didn't arrive until six months later and it brought no good news. Madison signed the official declaration of war with England on June 18, 1812. In August, he learned that Great Britain had yielded and repealed its Orders in Council. Unfortunately, it took the news two months to get to the U.S. The Orders had been revoked on June 17, 1812, just one day before Madison declared war! Had travel been faster, had communication been easier, the news would have been enough to prevent the war.

The victory of the *Constitution* over the *Guerrière* in the War of 1812. The *Constitution* was nicknamed "Old Ironsides" because its oak hull withstood so much bombardment. Now docked in Boston, the *Constitution* is the world's oldest warship still afloat.

Chapter 9

The War of 1812

The United States' best strategy was to move quickly to capture British Canada. A victory there might force Great Britain to settle America's other grievances. Unfortunately, the army's first tries ended in humiliating defeats. The U.S. had no warships on the Great Lakes to support land attacks. The army was poorly trained and led by bungling generals.

In Detroit, General William Hull surrendered his force of 2,500 men to a British force of 700 without firing a single shot. General Alexander Smyth roused his troops by shouting "Come on my heroes!" He loaded his men into boats for an attack on British Fort Erie. Before launching the boats, he demanded that the fort surrender. When the British refused, Smyth unloaded the boats and ran for it before his own men could shoot him.

In spite of these fiascos, Madison was elected to a second term. The narrow margin of victory, 128 electoral votes for Madison to 89 votes for DeWitt Clinton, reflected how divided the country was over the war.

Instead of uniting against the enemy, the New England Federalists were coming close to rebellion. One Boston preacher said, "As Mr. Madison has declared war, let Mr. Madison carry it on. . . . The Union has long since virtually dissolved: and it is full time that this part of the Disunited States should take care of themselves." Federalist congressmen fought against raising taxes, forcing Madison's government to borrow millions of dollars to pay for the war. Federalist governors refused to send their state militias to protect the coast; Federalist traders made a profit smuggling supplies to the enemy.

When Madison lay deathly ill with a fever for several weeks in the summer of 1813, Federalist congressmen accused him of tricking the country into the war. They claimed that Madison was sick at the prospect of a congressional investigation. A Federalist newspaper reported that Napoleon had offered Madison a million francs and the presidency for life to make war on Great Britain. Overall, the Federalists hurt the American war effort, and worse yet, encouraged the British to keep fighting.

After the army's terrible losses, Madison replaced imcompetent generals with more daring and effective leaders, such as Winfield Scott and Andrew Jackson. He sent Commodore Isaac Chauncey to build up a Great Lakes fleet as fast as he could. Both the new ships and the new commanders got results.

In 1813, Oliver Hazard Perry won an astonishing naval victory on Lake Erie. He sailed his ship right through a squadron, firing broadsides all the way. Perry captured the entire squadron and won control of the lake.

Commodore Oliver Hazard Perry transfers from his sinking flagship *Lawrence* to the *Niagara* during the Battle of Lake Erie. After his victory he reported, "We have met the enemy and they are ours."

A few months later, Generals William Henry Harrison and Winfield Scott won battles that pushed the British and their allies, the Indians, out of the Michigan Territory. For the rest of the war, American troops were able to hold the line against the British in the north.

Throughout the War of 1812, Madison and the country were buoyed up by America's many naval victories. These victories were astonishing because the American navy was so severely outnumbered. The U.S. had only twenty-five warships to England's seven hundred. Madison was constantly urging Congress to spend money on shipbuilding.

Above: General William Henry Harrison routs Tecumseh's Indians in the Battle of Tippecanoe.
Below: The famous Indian leader Tecumseh meets his death in the Battle of the Thames.

Above: A soldier's wife lends a hand in the Battle of Fort Niagara. Below: Commandant Thomas Macdonough wipes out the British squadron at the Battle of Lake Champlain.

In November 1812, naval officers and lawmakers were mingling at a party when an officer brought good news— the American ship *United States* had just turned the *Macedonian*, the largest ship in the British navy, into "a perfect wreck and unmanageable log." Officers paraded the flag of the *Macedonian* around the party and laid it at Dolley Madison's feet. Soon afterward, Congress voted to build ten new ships.

Although the U.S. Navy won many victories, it did not have the ships or manpower to fight off a British blockade of the American coast. American ports from New York to the South were closed to trade by patrolling British war-ships. By 1814, Britain was eager to punish America for the war. The war against France was over, and suddenly Great Britain had thousands of tough, seasoned fighters to send into the war against the United States.

At just this time, the United States was ready to make peace. All the abuses that had forced Madison to declare war had abruptly stopped. Now that the European war was over, Britain no longer needed to force American sailors into service, and neither Britain nor France had any reason to harass American shipping. Madison sent peace commissioners to work on a treaty. Nevertheless, the United States had no choice but to keep on fighting.

Madison believed that an attack on Washington was becoming more and more likely. Secretary of War John Armstrong disagreed. Madison ordered Armstrong to summon ten thousand militiamen to defend the capital city. Armstrong stalled. He made no plan for the city's defense, set up no roadblocks, issued no emergency ammunition.

Seven weeks later, fifty British ships dropped anchor two days' march away from Washington. Four thousand British soldiers began a slow advance toward the capital. No one fired at them; no troops met them; not even one tree had been cut down to block the road.

Back in Washington, Armstrong noticed a clerk packing important documents, such as the Declaration of Independence, to get them out of the city. He told the clerk that he "did not think the British were serious in their intentions of coming to Washington." At midnight that same day, a messenger woke up the Madisons to warn them that the British were coming.

Madison rode out to help order the city's defenses early on August 24. He found tired, inexperienced militiamen. Their indecisive general had been marching them to different spots, trying to guess where they could best attack the advancing British. The militia was now separated and strung out into two lines of about two thousand men each. It was too late to rearrange anything now. Madison and his officers rode back behind the lines and saw that "the militia ran like sheep chased by dogs."

In the White House, Dolley Madison saved what she could. She knew that everything left behind would be destroyed, so she insisted on taking a full-length portrait of George Washington. The huge frame was screwed into the wall. Unscrewing it could take hours; the sounds of gunfire were coming closer and closer. She had a gardener crack the frame and sent the portrait out of Washington on a wagon along with the White House silver and a set of crimson velvet curtains. Then she set out a dinner for

Madison and left the city for their meeting point across the Potomac River.

Madison checked the White House to make certain his wife was safely away. Then he "coolly mounted his horse" and crossed by ferry into Virginia. When British Commander Cockburn reached the White House, he went inside and drank an irreverent toast to "Jemmy's health." ("Jemmy" was Madison's childhood nickname.) Then he sat down and ate the dinner Dolley had set out for her husband. Next, Cockburn's men surrounded the White House and started a fire at every window with torches.

Above: Residents scramble as the British torch Washington, D.C.
Opposite page: Dolley Madison flees the flaming capital.

As President Madison rode away from his capital, he saw "columns of flame and smoke ascending throughout the night . . . from the Capitol, the President's house, and other public edifices . . . some burning slowly, others with bursts of flame and sparks mounting high up."

Three days later, the British retreated. Madison rode back to find that all the city's public buildings except the Post Office and the Patent Office had been turned into a smoking heap of ashes. However, the British had left private houses alone, so the president and the first lady moved in with relatives. They had a guard of eleven soldiers, who slept outside at night on some straw. One of Madison's first acts after he returned was to dismiss Secretary of War Armstrong.

Seeing the American flag still waving over Fort McHenry,
Francis Scott Key writes "The Star-Spangled Banner."

Madison refused to move the government to a safer
place, even though the British fleet was still nearby. Congress could use the Post and Patent Offices. Other officials
could work from private homes. Within one month of the
British attack, the government was back in operation in
Washington. For the moment the war news was good. The
British were turned back in upper New York and at
Baltimore. All through the night of September 14, a young
man named Francis Scott Key watched British cannons fire
on Baltimore's Fort McHenry. Key was so relieved and
proud to see the American flag still flying over the fort the
next morning that he wrote the words to "The Star-
Spangled Banner."

The Star-spangled banner.

O say! can you see by the dawn's early light
What so proudly we hail'd at the twilight's last gleaming
Whose broad stripes and bright stars, through the clouds of the fight,
O'er the ramparts we watch'd were so gallantly streaming?
And the rocket's red glare - the bomb bursting in air
Gave proof through the night that our flag was still there?
O say, does that star-spangled banner yet wave
O'er the land of the free & the home of the brave? —

A copy of Francis Scott Key's original manuscript

Still, the British had not given up. They switched their attack to the South. If they could take New Orleans, they would be able to move up the Mississippi River. By now, the U.S. government needed $50 million to keep fighting the war. Congress delayed passing taxes for months. Meanwhile Madison put Andrew Jackson in charge of defending New Orleans against a British landing force of ten thousand soldiers. Jackson had six thousand men, including Jean Lafitte and his pirates.

Jackson fought the British on January 8, 1815. Madison waited anxiously for news of the outcome for almost a month. The Federalists claimed that Madison was afraid to tell the country about a defeat. They sent a delegation to Washington to force Madison to resign. Their disloyalty was coming close to treason. But on February 4, Madison

Unaware that the war has been over for two weeks, General Andrew Jackson fights the Battle of New Orleans.

finally learned about Jackson's incredible victory. The Americans had taken cover between the Mississippi River and a swamp. When the British marched at them they opened fire. The British gave up after losing seven hundred men. The Americans lost seven.

On February 14, there was more good news. Great Britain had agreed to a peace treaty. The Prince Regent had signed it before the Battle of New Orleans. Madison was surprised and elated. Congress voted within one day to accept the treaty. On February 17, 1815, Madison declared that the war was over. Everyone except the Federalists rejoiced; their party's power was broken for good. Thomas Jefferson wrote that in any other country, the Federalists'

The Treaty of Ghent ends the War of 1812 on December 24, 1814.
American delegate John Quincy Adams is shown shaking hands with
British delegate Lord Gambier.

disloyalty and resistance during the war would have been
grounds for hanging. "We let them live as the laughing
stocks of the world, and punish them by the torment of
eternal contempt."

For Madison this may have been the greatest achieve-
ment of the war—he never tried to limit the personal
liberties of even the most rebellious citizens. The mayor of
Washington summed up the way Madison conducted the
war: "Power and national glory, sir, have often before
been acquired by the sword; but rarely without the
sacrifice of civil or political liberty. . . . You have wielded
an armed force of fifty thousand men . . . without infring-
ing a political, civil or religious right."

Chapter 10

Retirement

The good feeling left by the war lasted throughout Madison's last year in the White House. For the first time in his presidency, Madison had an easy working relationship with Congress. As Madison requested, Congress voted to maintain a standing army and navy and keep war taxes to help pay the national debt. His friend James Monroe easily won the presidential election of 1816.

Dolley Madison began sending wagonloads of their belongings home to Virginia. The last of the Madisons' Wednesday receptions were jammed with all kinds of people, "members of Congress and officers of the army and navy, greasy boots and silk stockings, Virginia buckskins and Yankee cowhides, all mingled."

After Monroe's inauguration in 1817, the Madisons stayed in Washington for a month of farewell celebrations. Even former President John Adams said that Madison's presidency "acquired more glory, and established more Union, than all three predecessors, Washington, Adams and Jefferson, put together." Finally, the Madisons left for Montpelier. Only this time, instead of traveling by carriage or on horseback as Madison had done fifty years before, they boarded a steamboat for the first forty miles.

Opposite: One of the Madisons' weekly receptions at the White House

85

Once at home, the Madisons entertained a constant stream of visitors. Madison took up the life of a planter, riding around on his horse, Liberty, to check on his crops every day. Sometimes guests rode with him. One visitor remembered Madison leaning from horseback and opening gates with a crooked stick, "a feat which required no little skill." Another described the ex-president at home: "A short thin man . . . he has gray but bright eyes, and small features. . . . The expression of his face is full of good humour — he was dressed in black, with breeches and old fashioned top boots, which he afterwards took off and sat during the evening in his white stockings."

Now Madison had time to spend in his second-floor library. Over the years, he had amassed a collection of four thousand books in various languages. (Madison could read in Greek, Latin, French, Italian, Spanish, and Hebrew.) In the evenings, the Madisons strolled with their guests on the broad front porch and drank coffee in a drawing room filled with paintings of great American statesmen. The chief entertainment was always Madison's conversation.

Although he never returned to Washington, he was drawn back into public issues by the very respect everyone had for him. President Monroe routinely sent Madison copies of official documents and asked his opinion. In 1829, Virginia called a convention to write a new state constitution. Madison was elected as delegate from his county. He was the only delegate who had been present at the first Virginia convention back in 1776. When the convention ended, all the delegates crowded around to shake Madison's hand.

When a dispute between the southern states and the northern states broke out in 1828, both sides quoted from Madison's writings to support their arguments. Congress had set up a tariff system of import duties to protect American-made goods from cheaper foreign products. South Carolina and Virginia were angry because they had to pay the higher prices so that the northern manufacturing states could make a profit. South Carolina nullified the tariff—it refused to pay it.

This worried Madison. If states could refuse to follow any federal laws that they didn't like, the Union would soon fall to pieces. Worse yet, South Carolina was using Madison's own words to support nullification.

Madison didn't want anyone to believe that he was on the side of the nullifiers: "What *madness* in the South to look for greater safety in disunion. It would be worse than jumping out of the Frying-pan into the fire: it would be jumping into the fire for fear of the Frying-pan." In spite of rheumatism in his hands, the seventy-nine-year-old Madison took up the task of writing a reply.

Madison kept friends in Congress and the government supplied with arguments and historical information to prove that "whilst a State remains within the Union it cannot withdraw its citizens from the operation of the Constitution and laws of the Union." In 1833, a compromise tariff bill satisfied the southern states and ended the crisis. Once again, Madison's understanding of the Constitution and his vision of republican government had helped to preserve the Union. This was the last time Madison took an active part in national affairs.

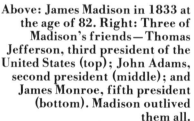

Above: James Madison in 1833 at
the age of 82. Right: Three of
Madison's friends — Thomas
Jefferson, third president of the
United States (top); John Adams,
second president (middle); and
James Monroe, fifth president
(bottom). Madison outlived
them all.

Off and on after 1831, writing was very difficult for
Madison. Rheumatism stiffened his wrists until he could
move only his fingertips. Madison began arranging his
papers and letters, putting his records of the past in order.
Historians sought him out to ask questions about the
founding of the United States and about the great men
Madison had known.

By 1831, Madison had outlived all of his friends from
the early days. In August 1825, Jefferson, Madison, and
Monroe gathered at Jefferson's home to meet with the
French General Marquis de Lafayette on his farewell tour

of the U.S. (Lafayette had gallantly fought for America back in the revolutionary war.) This was the last time Madison saw Thomas Jefferson, his friend of fifty years. Jefferson died on July 4, 1826. Madison wrote, "I have known him . . . for a period of fifty years, during which there has not been an interruption or diminution of mutual confidence and cordial friendship, for a single moment in a single instance."

On July 4, 1831, another close friend, James Monroe, died in New York. Madison wrote, "Having outlived so many of my contemporaries, I ought not to forget that I may be thought to have outlived myself." As Madison's health grew worse and worse, some people suggested that he should try to hold on until the Fourth of July, since three former presidents, Adams, Jefferson, and Monroe, had all died on that date. Madison did not take their advice. He died calmly at breakfast on June 28, 1836.

The entire country mourned Madison. He had had the intelligence and vision to help form a new kind of republic, as well as the patience, firmness, and foresight to keep the good of that republic in mind through crisis after crisis. Fortunately for the United States, Madison was a man of great abilities who found a great task. After forty years of public service—in the Continental Congress, the Constitutional Convention, Congress, the cabinet, and the presidency—he was not disillusioned. During his retirement he wrote: "The happy Union of these states is a wonder; their constitution is miracle, their example the hope of Liberty throughout the world. Woe to the ambition that would meditate the destruction of either!"

Chronology of American History

(Shaded area covers events in James Madison's lifetime.)

About A.D. 982—Eric the Red, born in Norway, reaches Greenland in one of the first European voyages to North America.

About 1000—Leif Ericson (Eric the Red's son) leads what is thought to be the first European expedition to mainland North America; Leif probably lands in Canada.

1492—Christopher Columbus, seeking a sea route from Spain to the Far East, discovers the New World.

1497—John Cabot reaches Canada in the first English voyage to North America.

1513—Ponce de Léon explores Florida in search of the fabled Fountain of Youth.

1519-1521—Hernando Cortés of Spain conquers Mexico.

1534—French explorers led by Jacques Cartier enter the Gulf of St. Lawrence in Canada.

1540—Spanish explorer Francisco Coronado begins exploring the American Southwest, seeking the riches of the mythical Seven Cities of Cibola.

1565—St. Augustine, Florida, the first permanent European town in what is now the United States, is founded by the Spanish.

1607—Jamestown, Virginia, is founded, the first permanent English town in the present-day U.S.

1608—Frenchman Samuel de Champlain founds the village of Quebec, Canada.

1609—Henry Hudson explores the eastern coast of present-day U.S. for the Netherlands; the Dutch then claim parts of New York, New Jersey, Delaware, and Connecticut and name the area New Netherland.

1619—The English colonies' first shipment of black slaves arrives in Jamestown.

1620—English Pilgrims found Massachusetts's first permanent town at Plymouth.

1621—Massachusetts Pilgrims and Indians hold the famous first Thanksgiving feast in colonial America.

1623—Colonization of New Hampshire is begun by the English.

1624—Colonization of present-day New York State is begun by the Dutch at Fort Orange (Albany).

1625—The Dutch start building New Amsterdam (now New York City).

1630—The town of Boston, Massachusetts, is founded by the English Puritans.

1633—Colonization of Connecticut is begun by the English.

1634—Colonization of Maryland is begun by the English.

1636—Harvard, the colonies' first college, is founded in Massachusetts. Rhode Island colonization begins when Englishman Roger Williams founds Providence.

1638—Delaware colonization begins as Swedes build Fort Christina at present-day Wilmington.

1640—Stephen Daye of Cambridge, Massachusetts, prints *The Bay Psalm Book*, the first English-language book published in what is now the U.S.

1643—Swedish settlers begin colonizing Pennsylvania.

About 1650—North Carolina is colonized by Virginia settlers.

1660—New Jersey colonization is begun by the Dutch at present-day Jersey City.

1670—South Carolina colonization is begun by the English near Charleston.

1673—Jacques Marquette and Louis Jolliet explore the upper Mississippi River for France.

1682—Philadelphia, Pennsylvania, is settled. La Salle explores Mississippi River all the way to its mouth in Louisiana and claims the whole Mississippi Valley for France.

1693—College of William and Mary is founded in Williamsburg, Virginia.

1700—Colonial population is about 250,000.

1703—Benjamin Franklin is born in Boston.

1732—George Washington, first president of the U.S., is born in Westmoreland County, Virginia.

1733—James Oglethorpe founds Savannah, Georgia; Georgia is established as the thirteenth colony.

1735—John Adams, second president of the U.S., is born in Braintree, Massachusetts.

1737—William Byrd founds Richmond, Virginia.

1738—British troops are sent to Georgia over border dispute with Spain.

1739—Black insurrection takes place in South Carolina.

1740—English Parliament passes act allowing naturalization of immigrants to American colonies after seven-year residence.

1743—Thomas Jefferson is born in Albemarle County, Virginia. Benjamin Franklin retires at age thirty-seven to devote himself to scientific inquiries and public service.

1744—King George's War begins; France joins war effort against England.

1745—During King George's War, France raids settlements in Maine and New York.

1747—Classes begin at Princeton College in New Jersey.

1748—The Treaty of Aix-la-Chapelle concludes King George's War.

1749—Parliament legally recognizes slavery in colonies and the inauguration of the plantation system in the South. George Washington becomes the surveyor for Culpepper County in Virginia.

1750—Thomas Walker passes through and names Cumberland Gap on his way toward Kentucky region. Colonial population is about 1,200,000.

1751—James Madison, fourth president of the U.S., is born in Port Conway, Virginia. English Parliament passes Currency Act, banning New England colonies from issuing paper money. George Washington travels to Barbados.

1752—Pennsylvania Hospital, the first general hospital in the colonies, is founded in Philadelphia. Benjamin Franklin uses a kite in a thunderstorm to demonstrate that lightning is a form of electricity.

1753—George Washington delivers command that the French withdraw from the Ohio River Valley; French disregard the demand. Colonial population is about 1,328,000.

1754—French and Indian War begins (extends to Europe as the Seven Years' War). Washington surrenders at Fort Necessity.

1755—French and Indians ambush Braddock. Washington becomes commander of Virginia troops.

1756—England declares war on France.

1758—James Monroe, fifth president of the U.S., is born in Westmoreland County, Virginia.

1759—Cherokee Indian war begins in southern colonies; hostilities extend to 1761. George Washington marries Martha Dandridge Custis.

1760—George III becomes king of England. Colonial population is about 1,600,000.

1762—England declares war on Spain.

1763—Treaty of Paris concludes the French and Indian War and the Seven Years' War. England gains Canada and most other French lands east of the Mississippi River.

1764—British pass the Sugar Act to gain tax money from the colonists. The issue of taxation without representation is first introduced in Boston. John Adams marries Abigail Smith.

1765—Stamp Act goes into effect in the colonies. Business virtually stops as almost all colonists refuse to use the stamps.

1766—British repeal the Stamp Act.

1767—John Quincy Adams, sixth president of the U.S. and son of second president John Adams, is born in Braintree, Massachusetts. Andrew Jackson, seventh president of the U.S., is born in Waxhaw settlement, South Carolina.

1769—Daniel Boone sights the Kentucky Territory.

1770—In the Boston Massacre, British soldiers kill five colonists and injure six. Townshend Acts are repealed, thus eliminating all duties on imports to the colonies except tea.

1771—Benjamin Franklin begins his autobiography, a work that he will never complete. The North Carolina assembly passes the "Bloody Act," which makes rioters guilty of treason.

1772—Samuel Adams rouses colonists to consider British threats to self-government.

1773—English Parliament passes the Tea Act. Colonists dressed as Mohawk Indians board British tea ships and toss 342 casks of tea into the water in what becomes known as the Boston Tea Party. William Henry Harrison is born in Charles City County, Virginia.

1774—British close the port of Boston to punish the city for the Boston Tea Party. First Continental Congress convenes in Philadelphia.

1775—American Revolution begins with battles of Lexington and Concord, Massachusetts. Second Continental Congress opens in Philadelphia. George Washington becomes commander-in-chief of the Continental army.

1776—Declaration of Independence is adopted on July 4.

1777—Congress adopts the American flag with thirteen stars and thirteen stripes. John Adams is sent to France to negotiate peace treaty.

1778—France declares war against Great Britain and becomes U.S. ally.

1779—British surrender to Americans at Vincennes. Thomas Jefferson is elected governor of Virginia. James Madison is elected to the Continental Congress.

1780—Benedict Arnold, first American traitor, defects to the British.

1781—Articles of Confederation go into effect. Cornwallis surrenders to George Washington at Yorktown, ending the American Revolution.

1782—American commissioners, including John Adams, sign peace treaty with British in Paris. Thomas Jefferson's wife, Martha, dies. Martin Van Buren is born in Kinderhook, New York.

1784—Zachary Taylor is born near Barboursville, Virginia.

1785—Congress adopts the dollar as the unit of currency. John Adams is made minister to Great Britain. Thomas Jefferson is appointed minister to France.

1786—Shays's Rebellion begins in Massachusetts.

1787—Constitutional Convention assembles in Philadelphia, with George Washington presiding; U.S. Constitution is adopted. Delaware, New Jersey, and Pennsylvania become states.

1788—Virginia, South Carolina, New York, Connecticut, New Hampshire, Maryland, and Massachusetts become states. U.S. Constitution is ratified. New York City is declared U.S. capital.

1789—Presidential electors elect George Washington and John Adams as first president and vice-president. Thomas Jefferson is appointed secretary of state. North Carolina becomes a state. French Revolution begins.

1790—Supreme Court meets for the first time. Rhode Island becomes a state. First national census in the U.S. counts 3,929,214 persons. John Tyler is born in Charles City County, Virginia.

1791—Vermont enters the Union. U.S. Bill of Rights, the first ten amendments to the Constitution, goes into effect. District of Columbia is established. James Buchanan is born in Stony Batter, Pennsylvania.

1792—Thomas Paine publishes *The Rights of Man*. Kentucky becomes a state. Two political parties are formed in the U.S., Federalist and Republican. Washington is elected to a second term, with Adams as vice-president.

1793—War between France and Britain begins; U.S. declares neutrality. Eli Whitney invents the cotton gin; cotton production and slave labor increase in the South.

1794—Eleventh Amendment to the Constitution is passed, limiting federal courts' power. "Whiskey Rebellion" in Pennsylvania protests federal whiskey tax. James Madison marries Dolley Payne Todd.

1795—George Washington signs the Jay Treaty with Great Britain. Treaty of San Lorenzo, between U.S. and Spain, settles Florida boundary and gives U.S. right to navigate the Mississippi. James Polk is born near Pineville, North Carolina.

1796—Tennessee enters the Union. Washington gives his Farewell Address, refusing a third presidential term. John Adams is elected president and Thomas Jefferson vice-president.

1797—Adams recommends defense measures against possible war with France. Napoleon Bonaparte and his army march against Austrians in Italy. U.S. population is about 4,900,000.

1798—Washington is named commander-in-chief of the U.S. Army. Department of the Navy is created. Alien and Sedition Acts are passed. Napoleon's troops invade Egypt and Switzerland.

1799—George Washington dies at Mount Vernon, New York. James Monroe is elected governor of Virginia. French Revolution ends. Napoleon becomes ruler of France.

1800—Thomas Jefferson and Aaron Burr tie for president. U.S. capital is moved from Philadelphia to Washington, D.C. The White House is built as presidents' home. Spain returns Louisiana to France. Millard Fillmore is born in Locke, New York.

1801—After thirty-six ballots, House of Representatives elects Thomas Jefferson president, making Burr vice-president. James Madison is named secretary of state.

1802—Congress abolishes excise taxes. U.S. Military Academy is founded at West Point, New York.

1803—Ohio enters the Union. Louisiana Purchase treaty is signed with France, greatly expanding U.S. territory.

1804—Twelfth Amendment to the Constitution rules that president and vice-president be elected separately. Alexander Hamilton is killed by Vice-President Aaron Burr in a duel. Orleans Territory is established. Napoleon crowns himself emperor of France. Franklin Pierce is born in Hillsborough Lower Village, New Hampshire.

1805—Thomas Jefferson begins his second term as president. Lewis and Clark expedition reaches the Pacific Ocean.

1806—Coinage of silver dollars is stopped; resumes in 1836.

1807—Aaron Burr is acquitted in treason trial. Embargo Act closes U.S. ports to trade.

1808—James Madison is elected president. Congress outlaws importing slaves from Africa. Andrew Johnson is born in Raleigh, North Carolina.

1809—Abraham Lincoln is born near Hodgenville, Kentucky.

1810—U.S. population is 7,240,000.

1811—William Henry Harrison defeats Indians at Tippecanoe. Monroe is named secretary of state.

1812—Louisiana becomes a state. U.S. declares war on Britain (War of 1812). James Madison is reelected president. Napoleon invades Russia.

1813—British forces take Fort Niagara and Buffalo, New York.

1814—Francis Scott Key writes "The Star-Spangled Banner." British troops burn much of Washington, D.C., including the White House. Treaty of Ghent ends War of 1812. James Monroe becomes secretary of war.

1815—Napoleon meets his final defeat at Battle of Waterloo.

1816—James Monroe is elected president. Indiana becomes a state.

1817—Mississippi becomes a state. Construction on Erie Canal begins.

1818—Illinois enters the Union. The present thirteen-stripe flag is adopted. Border between U.S. and Canada is agreed upon.

1819—Alabama becomes a state. U.S. purchases Florida from Spain. Thomas Jefferson establishes the University of Virginia.

1820—James Monroe is reelected. In the Missouri Compromise, Maine enters the Union as a free (non-slave) state.

1821—Missouri enters the Union as a slave state. Santa Fe Trail opens the American Southwest. Mexico declares independence from Spain. Napoleon Bonaparte dies.

1822—U.S. recognizes Mexico and Colombia. Liberia in Africa is founded as a home for freed slaves. Ulysses S. Grant is born in Point Pleasant, Ohio. Rutherford B. Hayes is born in Delaware, Ohio.

1823—Monroe Doctrine closes North and South America to European colonizing or invasion.

1824—House of Representatives elects John Quincy Adams president when none of the four candidates wins a majority in national election. Mexico becomes a republic.

1825—Erie Canal is opened. U.S. population is 11,300,000.

1826—Thomas Jefferson and John Adams both die on July 4, the fiftieth anniversary of the Declaration of Independence.

1828—Andrew Jackson is elected president. Tariff of Abominations is passed, cutting imports.

1829—James Madison attends Virginia's constitutional convention. Slavery is abolished in Mexico. Chester A. Arthur is born in Fairfield, Vermont.

1830—Indian Removal Act to resettle Indians west of the Mississippi is approved.

1831—James Monroe dies in New York City. James A. Garfield is born in Orange, Ohio. Cyrus McCormick develops his reaper.

1832—Andrew Jackson, nominated by the new Democratic Party, is reelected president.

1833—Britain abolishes slavery in its colonies. Benjamin Harrison is born in North Bend, Ohio.

1835—Federal government becomes debt-free for the first time.

1836—Martin Van Buren becomes president. Texas wins independence from Mexico. Arkansas joins the Union. James Madison dies at Montpelier, Virginia.

1837—Michigan enters the Union. U.S. population is 15,900,000. Grover Cleveland is born in Caldwell, New Jersey.

1840—William Henry Harrison is elected president.

1841—President Harrison dies in Washington, D.C., one month after inauguration. Vice-President John Tyler succeeds him.

1843—William McKinley is born in Niles, Ohio.

1844—James Knox Polk is elected president. Samuel Morse sends first telegraphic message.

1845—Texas and Florida become states. Potato famine in Ireland causes massive emigration from Ireland to U.S. Andrew Jackson dies near Nashville, Tennessee.

1846—Iowa enters the Union. War with Mexico begins.

1847—U.S. captures Mexico City.

1848—John Quincy Adams dies in Washington, D.C. Zachary Taylor becomes president. Treaty of Guadalupe Hidalgo ends Mexico-U.S. war. Wisconsin becomes a state.

1849—James Polk dies in Nashville, Tennessee.

1850—President Taylor dies in Washington, D.C.; Vice-President Millard Fillmore succeeds him. California enters the Union, breaking tie between slave and free states.

1852—Franklin Pierce is elected president.

1853—Gadsden Purchase transfers Mexican territory to U.S.

1854—"War for Bleeding Kansas" is fought between slave and free states.

1855—Czar Nicholas I of Russia dies, succeeded by Alexander II.

1856—James Buchanan is elected president. In Massacre of Potawatomi Creek, Kansas-slavers are murdered by free-staters. Woodrow Wilson is born in Staunton, Virginia.

1857—William Howard Taft is born in Cincinnati, Ohio.

1858—Minnesota enters the Union. Theodore Roosevelt is born in New York City.

1859—Oregon becomes a state.

1860—Abraham Lincoln is elected president; South Carolina secedes from the Union in protest.

1861—Arkansas, Tennessee, North Carolina, and Virginia secede. Kansas enters the Union as a free state. Civil War begins.

1862—Union forces capture Fort Henry, Roanoke Island, Fort Donelson, Jacksonville, and New Orleans; Union armies are defeated at the battles of Bull Run and Fredericksburg. Martin Van Buren dies in Kinderhook, New York. John Tyler dies near Charles City, Virginia.

1863—Lincoln issues Emancipation Proclamation: all slaves held in rebelling territories are declared free. West Virginia becomes a state.

1864—Abraham Lincoln is reelected. Nevada becomes a state.

1865—Lincoln is assassinated in Washington, D.C., and succeeded by Andrew Johnson. U.S. Civil War ends on May 26. Thirteenth Amendment abolishes slavery. Warren G. Harding is born in Blooming Grove, Ohio.

1867—Nebraska becomes a state. U.S. buys Alaska from Russia for $7,200,000. Reconstruction Acts are passed.

1868—President Johnson is impeached for violating Tenure of Office Act, but is acquitted by Senate. Ulysses S. Grant is elected president. Fourteenth Amendment prohibits voting discrimination. James Buchanan dies in Lancaster, Pennsylvania.

1869—Franklin Pierce dies in Concord, New Hampshire.

1870—Fifteenth Amendment gives blacks the right to vote.

1872—Grant is reelected over Horace Greeley. General Amnesty Act pardons ex-Confederates. Calvin Coolidge is born in Plymouth Notch, Vermont.

1874—Millard Fillmore dies in Buffalo, New York. Herbert Hoover is born in West Branch, Iowa.

1875—Andrew Johnson dies in Carter's Station, Tennessee.

1876—Colorado enters the Union. "Custer's last stand": he and his men are massacred by Sioux Indians at Little Big Horn, Montana.

1877—Rutherford B. Hayes is elected president as all disputed votes are awarded to him.

1880—James A. Garfield is elected president.

1881—President Garfield is assassinated and dies in Elberon, New Jersey. Vice-President Chester A. Arthur succeeds him.

1882—U.S. bans Chinese immigration. Franklin D. Roosevelt is born in Hyde Park, New York.

1884—Grover Cleveland is elected president. Harry S. Truman is born in Lamar, Missouri.

1885—Ulysses S. Grant dies in Mount McGregor, New York.

1886—Statue of Liberty is dedicated. Chester A. Arthur dies in New York City.

1888—Benjamin Harrison is elected president.

1889—North Dakota, South Dakota, Washington, and Montana become states.

1890—Dwight D. Eisenhower is born in Denison, Texas. Idaho and Wyoming become states.

1892—Grover Cleveland is elected president.

1893—Rutherford B. Hayes dies in Fremont, Ohio.

1896—William McKinley is elected president. Utah becomes a state.

1898—U.S. declares war on Spain over Cuba.

1900—McKinley is reelected. Boxer Rebellion against foreigners in China begins.

1901—McKinley is assassinated by anarchist Leon Czolgosz in Buffalo, New York; Theodore Roosevelt becomes president. Benjamin Harrison dies in Indianapolis, Indiana.

1902—U.S. acquires perpetual control over Panama Canal.

1903—Alaskan frontier is settled.

1904—Russian-Japanese War breaks out. Theodore Roosevelt wins presidential election.

1905 — Treaty of Portsmouth signed, ending Russian-Japanese War.

1906 — U.S. troops occupy Cuba.

1907 — President Roosevelt bars all Japanese immigration. Oklahoma enters the Union.

1908 — William Howard Taft becomes president. Grover Cleveland dies in Princeton, New Jersey. Lyndon B. Johnson is born near Stonewall, Texas.

1909 — NAACP is founded under W.E.B. DuBois

1910 — China abolishes slavery.

1911 — Chinese Revolution begins. Ronald Reagan is born in Tampico, Illinois.

1912 — Woodrow Wilson is elected president. Arizona and New Mexico become states.

1913 — Federal income tax is introduced in U.S. through the Sixteenth Amendment. Richard Nixon is born in Yorba Linda, California. Gerald Ford is born in Omaha, Nebraska.

1914 — World War I begins.

1915 — British liner *Lusitania* is sunk by German submarine.

1916 — Wilson is reelected president.

1917 — U.S. breaks diplomatic relations with Germany. Czar Nicholas of Russia abdicates as revolution begins. U.S. declares war on Austria-Hungary. John F. Kennedy is born in Brookline, Massachusetts.

1918 — Wilson proclaims "Fourteen Points" as war aims. On November 11, armistice is signed between Allies and Germany.

1919 — Eighteenth Amendment prohibits sale and manufacture of intoxicating liquors. Wilson presides over first League of Nations; wins Nobel Peace Prize. Theodore Roosevelt dies in Oyster Bay, New York.

1920 — Nineteenth Amendment (women's suffrage) is passed. Warren Harding is elected president.

1921 — Adolf Hitler's stormtroopers begin to terrorize political opponents.

1922 — Irish Free State is established. Soviet states form USSR. Benito Mussolini forms Fascist government in Italy.

1923 — President Harding dies in San Francisco, California; he is succeeded by Vice-President Calvin Coolidge.

1924 — Coolidge is elected president. Woodrow Wilson dies in Washington, D.C. James Carter is born in Plains, Georgia. George Bush is born in Milton, Massachusetts.

1925 — Hitler reorganizes Nazi Party and publishes first volume of *Mein Kampf.*

1926 — Fascist youth organizations founded in Germany and Italy. Republic of Lebanon proclaimed.

1927 — Stalin becomes Soviet dictator. Economic conference in Geneva attended by fifty-two nations.

1928 — Herbert Hoover is elected president. U.S. and many other nations sign Kellogg-Briand pacts to outlaw war.

1929 — Stock prices in New York crash on "Black Thursday"; the Great Depression begins.

1930 — Bank of U.S. and its many branches close (most significant bank failure of the year). William Howard Taft dies in Washington, D.C.

1931 — Emigration from U.S. exceeds immigration for first time as Depression deepens.

1932 — Franklin D. Roosevelt wins presidential election in a Democratic landslide.

1933 — First concentration camps are erected in Germany. U.S. recognizes USSR and resumes trade. Twenty-First Amendment repeals prohibition. Calvin Coolidge dies in Northampton, Massachusetts.

1934 — Severe dust storms hit Plains states. President Roosevelt passes U.S. Social Security Act.

1936 — Roosevelt is reelected. Spanish Civil War begins. Hitler and Mussolini form Rome-Berlin Axis.

1937 — Roosevelt signs Neutrality Act.

1938 — Roosevelt sends appeal to Hitler and Mussolini to settle European problems amicably.

1939 — Germany takes over Czechoslovakia and invades Poland, starting World War II.

1940—Roosevelt is reelected for a third term.

1941—Japan bombs Pearl Harbor, U.S. declares war on Japan. Germany and Italy declare war on U.S.; U.S. then declares war on them.

1942—Allies agree not to make separate peace treaties with the enemies. U.S. government transfers more than 100,000 Nisei (Japanese-Americans) from west coast to inland concentration camps.

1943—Allied bombings of Germany begin.

1944—Roosevelt is reelected for a fourth term. Allied forces invade Normandy on D-Day.

1945—President Franklin D. Roosevelt dies in Warm Springs, Georgia; Vice-President Harry S. Truman succeeds him. Mussolini is killed; Hitler commits suicide. Germany surrenders. U.S. drops atomic bomb on Hiroshima; Japan surrenders: end of World War II.

1946—U.N. General Assembly holds its first session in London. Peace conference of twenty-one nations is held in Paris.

1947—Peace treaties are signed in Paris. "Cold War" is in full swing.

1948—U.S. passes Marshall Plan Act, providing $17 billion in aid for Europe. U.S. recognizes new nation of Israel. India and Pakistan become free of British rule. Truman is elected president.

1949—Republic of Eire is proclaimed in Dublin. Russia blocks land route access from Western Germany to Berlin; airlift begins. U.S., France, and Britain agree to merge their zones of occupation in West Germany. Apartheid program begins in South Africa.

1950—Riots in Johannesburg, South Africa, against apartheid. North Korea invades South Korea. U.N. forces land in South Korea and recapture Seoul.

1951—Twenty-Second Amendment limits president to two terms.

1952—Dwight D. Eisenhower resigns as supreme commander in Europe and is elected president.

1953—Stalin dies; struggle for power in Russia follows. Rosenbergs are executed for espionage.

1954—U.S. and Japan sign mutual defense agreement.

1955—Blacks in Montgomery, Alabama, boycott segregated bus lines.

1956—Eisenhower is reelected president. Soviet troops march into Hungary.

1957—U.S. agrees to withdraw ground forces from Japan. Russia launches first satellite, *Sputnik.*

1958—European Common Market comes into being. Fidel Castro begins war against Batista government in Cuba.

1959—Alaska becomes the forty-ninth state. Hawaii becomes fiftieth state. Castro becomes premier of Cuba. De Gaulle is proclaimed president of the Fifth Republic of France.

1960—Historic debates between Senator John F. Kennedy and Vice-President Richard Nixon are televised. Kennedy is elected president. Brezhnev becomes president of USSR.

1961—Berlin Wall is constructed. Kennedy and Khrushchev confer in Vienna. In Bay of Pigs incident, Cubans trained by CIA attempt to overthrow Castro.

1962—U.S. military council is established in South Vietnam.

1963—Riots and beatings by police and whites mark civil rights demonstrations in Birmingham, Alabama; 30,000 troops are called out, Martin Luther King, Jr., is arrested. Freedom marchers descend on Washington, D.C., to demonstrate. President Kennedy is assassinated in Dallas, Texas; Vice-President Lyndon B. Johnson is sworn in as president.

1964—U.S. aircraft bomb North Vietnam. Johnson is elected president. Herbert Hoover dies in New York City.

1965—U.S. combat troops arrive in South Vietnam.

1966—Thousands protest U.S. policy in Vietnam. National Guard quells race riots in Chicago.

1967—Six-Day War between Israel and Arab nations.

1968—Martin Luther King, Jr., is assassinated in Memphis, Tennessee. Senator Robert Kennedy is assassinated in Los Angeles. Riots and police brutality take place at Democratic National Convention in Chicago. Richard Nixon is elected president. Czechoslovakia is invaded by Soviet troops.

1969—Dwight D. Eisenhower dies in Washington, D.C. Hundreds of thousands of people in several U.S. cities demonstrate against Vietnam War.

1970—Four Vietnam War protesters are killed by National Guardsmen at Kent State University in Ohio.

1971—Twenty-Sixth Amendment allows eighteen-year-olds to vote.

1972—Nixon visits Communist China; is reelected president in near-record landslide. Watergate affair begins when five men are arrested in the Watergate hotel complex in Washington, D.C. Nixon announces resignations of aides Haldeman, Ehrlichman, and Dean and Attorney General Kleindienst as a result of Watergate-related charges. Harry S. Truman dies in Kansas City, Missouri.

1973—Vice-President Spiro Agnew resigns; Gerald Ford is named vice-president. Vietnam peace treaty is formally approved after nineteen months of negotiations. Lyndon B. Johnson dies in San Antonio, Texas.

1974—As a result of Watergate cover-up, impeachment is considered; Nixon resigns and Ford becomes president. Ford pardons Nixon and grants limited amnesty to Vietnam War draft evaders and military deserters.

1975—U.S. civilians are evacuated from Saigon, South Vietnam, as Communist forces complete takeover of South Vietnam.

1976—U.S. celebrates its Bicentennial. James Earl Carter becomes president.

1977—Carter pardons most Vietnam draft evaders, numbering some 10,000.

1980—Ronald Reagan is elected president.

1981—President Reagan is shot in the chest in assassination attempt. Sandra Day O'Connor is appointed first woman justice of the Supreme Court.

1983—U.S. troops invade island of Grenada.

1984—Reagan is reelected president. Democratic candidate Walter Mondale's running mate, Geraldine Ferraro, is the first woman selected for vice-president by a major U.S. political party.

1985—Soviet Communist Party secretary Konstantin Chernenko dies; Mikhail Gorbachev succeeds him. U.S. and Soviet officials discuss arms control in Geneva. Reagan and Gorbachev hold summit conference in Geneva. Racial tensions accelerate in South Africa.

1986—Space shuttle *Challenger* explodes shortly after takeoff; crew of seven dies. U.S. bombs bases in Libya. Corazon Aquino defeats Ferdinand Marcos in Philippine presidential election.

1987—Iraqi missile rips the U.S. frigate *Stark* in the Persian Gulf, killing thirty-seven American sailors. Congress holds hearings to investigate sale of U.S. arms to Iran to finance Nicaraguan *contra* movement.

1988—President Reagan and Soviet leader Gorbachev sign INF treaty, eliminating intermediate nuclear forces. Severe drought sweeps the United States. George Bush is elected president.

1989—East Germany opens Berlin Wall, allowing citizens free exit. Communists lose control of governments in Poland, Romania, and Czechoslovakia. Chinese troops massacre over 1,000 pro-democracy student demonstrators in Beijing's Tiananmen Square.

1990—Iraq annexes Kuwait, provoking the threat of war. East and West Germany are reunited. The Cold War between the United States and the Soviet Union comes to a close. Several Soviet republics make moves toward independence.

1991—Backed by a coalition of members of the United Nations, U.S. troops drive Iraqis from Kuwait. Latvia, Lithuania, and Estonia withdraw from the USSR. The Soviet Union dissolves as its republics secede to form a Commonwealth of Independent States.

1992—U.N. forces fail to stop fighting in territories of former Yugoslavia. More than fifty people are killed and more than six hundred buildings burned in rioting in Los Angeles. U.S. unemployment reaches eight-year high. Hurricane Andrew devastates southern Florida and parts of Louisiana. International relief supplies and troops are sent to combat famine and violence in Somalia.

1993—U.S.-led forces use airplanes and missiles to attack military targets in Iraq. William Jefferson Clinton becomes the forty-second U.S. president.

1994—Richard M. Nixon dies in New York City.

Index

Page numbers in boldface type indicate illustrations.

Adams, John, 51-52, 54, 55, 85, **88**, 89
Adams, John Quincy, **83**
Alexandria, Virginia, **29**
American Revolution, 7, 10, **10**, 22-23, 31-32
Anglican church, 26-27
Armstrong, John, 76, 77, 79
Articles of Confederation, 7, 40, **42**, 43, 47, 50
Baltimore, Maryland, 80
Baptists, 27
Bedford, Gunning, 44
Bill for Religious Liberty, 29
Bill of Rights, 50
Blue Ridge Mountains, **14**, 15, 16
boycotts, 22
Brackenridge, Hugh Henry, 21
burning of Washington, D.C., 78-79, **79**
capital of U.S., 52, 53, 79-80
Charleston, South Carolina, **12**
Chauncey, Isaac, 72
Chesapeake (ship), 62
childhood, Madison's, 16-19
Christ Church (Alexandria, Virginia), **29**
Clinton, DeWitt, 71
Cockburn, Commander, 78
Congress, U.S., 50, 52, 65, 85, 87, 89
Connecticut, 36, 44
Constitution (ship), **70**
Constitution, U.S., **5**, **8**, **38**, 39-45, **45**, 47-50, 87
Constitutional Convention, 7-9, **9**, 11, 36-37, **38**, 39-45, 47, 89
Continental army, hardships of, 10, **10**, 31-32
Continental Congress, 10, 31-32, 34-37, 39, 43, 89
Continental currency, **30**, 31-32
death, Madison's, 89
Declaration of Independence, 7, 77
Delaware, 36, 43, 44
Democratic party, 52
Dunmore, Lord, 23
education, Madison's, 19-23
election, Madison's, 63, 71
embargo, 62-63, 65, 68
"Father of the Constitution," 9
Federalist, The, **46**, 47, **49**
Federalist party, 52, 53, 55, 60-61, 63, 65, 67-68, 72, 81-83
Fort Erie, 71

Fort McHenry, 80, **80**
Fort Niagara, Battle of, **75**
Foster, Augustus, 68
Franklin, Benjamin, 8, **8**, 30, 43
Freneau, Philip, 21, **21**
frontier life, 11, **11**
Gambier, Lord, **83**
Georgia, 35, 44
Gerry, Elbridge, 41
government, three branches of, 40
Guerrière (ship), **70**
Hamilton, Alexander, 8, **8**, 41, 47, 52
Harrison, William Henry, 73, **74**
Henry, Patrick, 26, 28, **28**, 35, 36, 48
Hornet (ship), 69
House of Representatives, 40, 43, 44, 50, 65
Hull, William, 71
illnesses, Madison's, 23, 72, 88
impressment, 62-63, **62**, 68
inauguration, Madison's, 65
inauguration, Monroe's, 85
inauguration, Washington's, **51**
Indian peace medal, **13**
Indians, 15, 73, 74
Jackson, Andrew, 72, 81-82, **82**
Jay, John, 47
Jefferson, Thomas, 29, 52, **53**, 55, 60, 62, 63, 65, 82-83, 85, 88, **88**, 89
Key, Francis Scott, 80, **80**
Knights of the Golden Horseshoe, 15
Lafayette, Marquis de, 88-89
Lafitte, Jean, 81
Lake Champlain, Battle of, **75**
Lake Erie, 15
Lake Erie, Battle of, 72, **73**
Lawrence (ship), **73**
Leopard (ship), 62
"logrolling," 35
Louisiana Purchase, 60-61, **61**
Macdonough, Thomas, **75**
Macedonian (ship), 76
Madison, Dolley, 18, 54, **56**, **57**, 76, 77-78, **78**, 85
Madison, James (illustrations): **2**, **6**, **24**; at age 82, **88**; at Constitutional Convention, **38**; giving Constitution to George Washington, **5**; on Indian peace medal, **13**; with Thomas Jefferson, **53**; in uniform, **23**; as a young man, **21**
marriage, Madison's, 54-55
Maryland, 44

Mason, George, 26-27, **26**, 48
Massachusetts, 36, 44
Mellimelli, Sidi Suliman, 59
money, U.S. problems in raising, 10, 31-37
Monroe, James, 50, 63, 67-68, 85, 86, 88, **88**, 89
Montpelier, 4, 18, **19**, 54, **55**, 85-86
Moore, William, 23
Morris, Robert, 32-33, **33**, **53**
Napoleon Bonaparte, 60, 61, 63, 66, 67, 72
National Archives, **5**
Navy, U.S., 73, 76
New Hampshire, 44
New Jersey, 19, 36, 43
New Jersey Plan, 43
New Orleans, Battle of, 81-82, **82**
New York, 35, 36, 44, 48, 50, 80
New York City, 52, 53
Niagara (ship), **73**
Norfolk (Virginia) Harbor, 23
North Carolina, 35, 44, 50
"Old Ironsides," **70**
Orange County, Virginia, 23, 27, 35
Orders in Council, 61, 63, 69
Paterson, William, 43
Pendleton, Edmund, 27
Pennsylvania, 36, 43, 44
Perry, Oliver Hazard, 72, **73**
Philadelphia, Pennsylvania, 7, 11, 32, 52, 53
physical appearance, Madison's, 8, 25
Pinckney, Charles, 63
political cartoons, **50**, **53**, **69**
Presbyterian church, 27
president, powers of, 40-41
president, title for, 51-52
Princeton College, 19-22, **20**
Randolph, Edmund, 39, 40, **41**
Randolph, John, 65
ratification of Constitution, 47-50, **50**
religious freedom, 26-29, 50
Republican party, 52, 55, 60, 63
retirement, Madison's, 85-89
Rhode Island, 33-34, 36, 44, 50
Robertson, Donald, 19
Salem, Massachusetts, **66**
Salomon, Haym, **33**

Scott, Winfield, 72, 73
secretary of state, Madison as, 55, 59-63
Senate, 40, 44
Sérurier, Louis, 67-68
settlers, **11**
Shays's Rebellion, 36, **37**, 40
Sherman, Roger, 44
slaves, 12, **12**, 16-17, **17**
Smith, Robert, 67
Smith, Samuel, 65, 67
Smyth, Alexander, 71
snuffboxes, 18, **18**
South Carolina, 35, 44, 87
Spotswood, Alexander, **14**, 15
Springfield, Massachusetts, **37**
"Star-Spangled Banner, The," 80, **81**
states vs. federal government, problems of, 7, 9, 10, 12, 31-37, 40-44, 87
taxation, by British, 22
taxation, for churches, 26-29
taxation, on imports, 32-36, 50, 87
Taylor, James, II, 16
Tecumseh, **74**
Thames, Battle of the, **74**
Tippecanoe, Battle of, **74**
tobacco industry, 12, 16, 18, **18**, 22, **22**, 35
Todd, Dolley Payne. *See* Madison, Dolley
travel, 11, 85
Treaty of Ghent (1814), 82, **83**
United States (ship), 76
Valley Forge, **10**
Virginia, 11, **14**, 15, 16, **16**, 22, 28, 32, 34, 35, 36, 37, 43, 44, 48, 85, 87
Virginia convention, 23, 25-29, 35, 86
Virginia Plan, 39-40, 41
war between England and France, 61-63, 66-68, 76
War of 1812, 69, **69**, **70**, 71-83, **73**, **74**, **75**, **80**, **82**
Washington, D.C., 53, **58**, 59, **64**, 76-80, **79**
Washington, George, **5**, 8, **8**, 39, 41, 51-52, **51**, 77, 85
White House, **58**, 59, 77-79, **84**, 85
William and Mary College, 19
Wilson, James, 41, **41**, 43
Witherspoon, John, 20

About the Author

Susan Clinton holds a Ph.D. in English and is a part-time teacher of English Literature at Northwestern University in Chicago. Her articles have appeared in such publications as *Consumer's Digest*, *Family Style Magazine*, and the Chicago *Reader*. In addition, she has been a contributor to *Encyclopaedia Britannica* and *Compton's Encyclopedia* and has written reader stories and other materials for a number of educational publishers. Her books for Childrens Press include *I Can Be an Architect* and *The Story of Susan B. Anthony*. Ms. Clinton lives in Chicago and is the mother of two boys.